THE BASICS OF

STATES OF MATTER

CORE CONCEPTS

THE BASICS OF

STATES OF MATTER

ANNE O'DALY

ROSEN PUBLISHING

Published in 2024 by The Rosen Publishing Group, Inc.
2544 Clinton Street, Buffalo, NY 14224

First edition published 2014. Second edition 2024.

Text and Editor: Lindsey Lowe
Children's Publisher: Anne O'Daly
Design Manager: Keith Davis
Manager: Lynn Lennon
Picture Manager: Sophie Mortimer
Consultant: Adrian Dingle

Cataloging-in-Publication Data

Names: O'Daly, Anne.
Title: The basics of states of matter / Anne O'Daly
Description: Second edition. | New York : Rosen Young Adult, 2024. | Series: Core concepts | Includes glossary and index.
Identifiers: ISBN 9781499475449 (pbk.) | ISBN 9781499475456 (library bound) | ISBN 9781499475463 (ebook)
Subjects: LCSH: Matter--Constitution--Juvenile literature. | Matter--Properties--Juvenile literature. | Change of state (Physics)--Juvenile literature.
Classification: LCC QC173.16 O34 2024 | DDC 530.4--dc23

Manufactured in the United States of America

CPSIA Compliance Information: Batch #CW24RYA. For further information, contact Rosen Publishing, New York, New York, at 1-800-237-9932.

Find us on

CONTENTS

CHAPTER 1

Solids, Liquids, and Gases

Everything is made from matter. Matter can exist in one of three basic forms, or states: as a solid, a liquid, or a gas. It can change states if energy is added or removed.

Water is one of the substances that can be seen in all three states of matter on Earth: as solid ice, as liquid water, and as gas in the form of water vapor.

All matter is made of tiny particles called atoms. When two or more atoms join, they form molecules. Atoms and molecules combine in different ways to form three types of matter—solids, liquids, and gases. These are called states of matter. The states of matter in which a particular substance can exist are called its phases. Water is a type of matter that we are all familiar with. What we call "water" is the matter's liquid phase. Its solid phase is called ice, and its gas phase is called vapor.

Solids

A solid is matter that has a definite shape and volume

(the space that a solid, liquid, or gas occupies). There are two main ways that a solid's particles can be arranged—in neat, ordered rows or in no particular order. Solids that have particles arranged in neatly ordered rows are described as crystalline. Common examples of crystalline solids are most metals, diamonds, ice, and salt. Solids with particles arranged in no specific order are described as amorphous. The texture of amorphous solids is usually described as being glassy or rubbery. Common examples of amorphous solids are wax, glass, rubber, and plastics. In all solids, the particles are closely packed together, so solids cannot easily be compressed—they cannot be made smaller by squeezing.

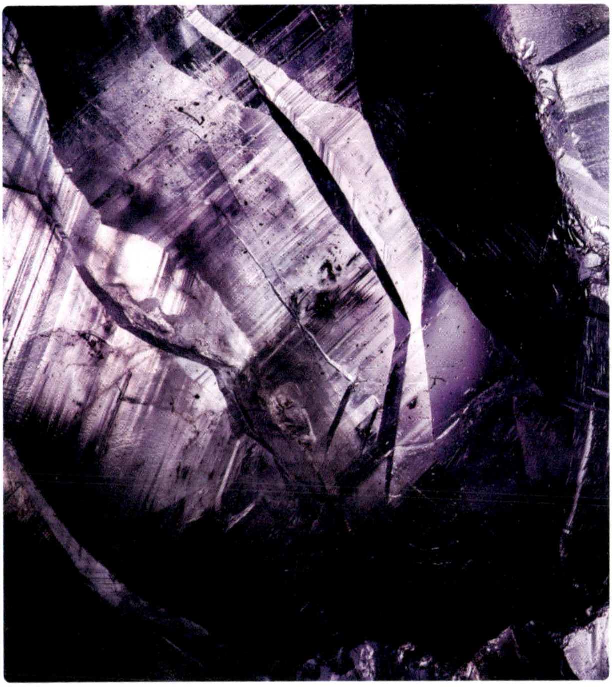

This purple amethyst has a crystalline structure—the atoms are arranged in neat, ordered rows.

Liquids

Like a solid, a liquid has a definite volume. Unlike a solid, a liquid will take the shape of the container it is poured into. Liquids are described as fluid. A fluid is a substance in which particles move freely past one another, so a fluid takes the shape of its container. Like solids, the particles in a liquid are close together. Liquids are also difficult to compress.

KEY TERMS

Kinetic energy: The energy of a moving particle.
Kinetic theory: Theory that describes the properties of matter in terms of the motion of particles.

Gases

Gas is a state of matter that easily changes its shape and volume. Like a liquid, a gas is described as fluid. The particles in a gas quickly spread out to fill all the available space. Because there are large distances between gas particles, gases can easily be compressed to reduce the volume.

THREE STATES OF MATTER

Solid

In a solid, individual particles do not move fast enough to overcome the attractive forces between the particles. The particles vibrate, but they are held firmly in place.

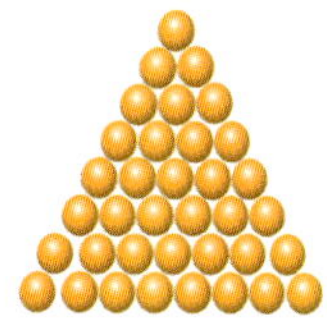

Liquid

In a liquid, particles are closely packed together. However, they have enough energy to overcome some of their attraction to their neighboring particles and slide past each other.

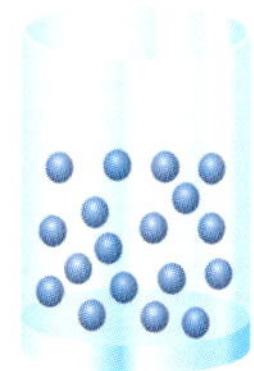

Gas

In a gas, individual particles move very fast, and they overcome almost all forces between particles. The particles move independently through the entire space in which they are contained.

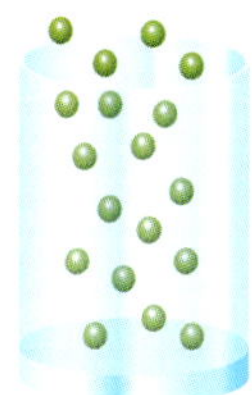

Particles in Motion

Kinetic theory describes the properties of matter in terms of the motion of particles. The particles in all matter are in constant motion. The energy of this motion is called kinetic energy. In solids, the particles are closely packed, and their motion is limited to vibrations. In a liquid, the particles are usually more widely spaced. They can vibrate but are also able to move freely throughout the liquid. In a gas, the particles are far apart and move randomly at high speeds.

According to kinetic theory, the faster a particle moves, the more energy it has. We experience this energy as heat. Something with fast-moving particles has a lot of energy, so it feels hot. Kinetic theory explains why a hot liquid poured into a cup causes the cup to heat up. The particles in a hot liquid are moving rapidly. As the particles in the liquid strike the surface of the cup, energy passes from the liquid to the cup. The particles in the cup then begin to vibrate. When we pick up a cup, energy from the cup's particles passes to our hand. We feel this energy as heat.

Robert Brown

The movement of molecules in liquids was discovered in 1827, when a Scottish botanist named Robert Brown began studying the movement of pollen grains in water. Brown observed the pollen grains moving randomly in the liquid. He then tried using pollen grains from plants that had been dead for more than a century. These grains showed the same random movement. The motion could not come from the grains themselves. Scientists now know that this movement is a result of rapidly moving water molecules colliding with the pollen grains. This type of movement is known as Brownian motion. In Brownian motion, minute particles suspended in a fluid will tend to spread out evenly throughout the fluid. Similar behavior occurs in gases. One example is the spread of a perfume across a room. Gas molecules in the air collide with perfume molecules. These collisions cause the perfume molecules to move randomly in all directions. Eventually, some of the molecules travel across the room and reach the smell sensors in your nose.

Internal Forces

Atoms are not the smallest pieces of matter. Atoms are made of smaller particles called protons, neutrons, and electrons. The center of an atom is called the nucleus and is made of protons and neutrons. Electrons are arranged around the nucleus in shells. Electrons and protons both have an electric charge. Electrons have a negative charge, and protons have a positive charge. Because their charges are opposite, electrons and protons are attracted to each other. The attractive forces hold electrons in place around the nucleus. These forces also hold atoms together in molecules.

The forces that hold atoms together in molecules are called intramolecular forces. Intra means "within." There are three main types of intramolecular forces. These are ionic bonds, covalent bonds, and metallic bonds. In ionic bonds, one atom gives its electrons to another atom. In covalent bonds, atoms share electrons. In metallic bonds, electrons move freely among atoms.

The forces that work between molecules are called intermolecular forces. These are the

↑ As food cooks, some of the molecules on the surface of the food are turned into gases. These molecules collide with gas molecules in the air and gradually spread over long distances. That is how you can tell when a neighbor farther down the street is having a barbecue!

TESTING: BROWNIAN MOTION

Materials:
glass
water
food coloring

1. Fill a tall glass with water and allow it to sit undisturbed for several hours.

2. Add one or two drops of food coloring to the water and watch how it spreads out. The particles of food coloring spread through the water because of collisions with water molecules. This movement is affected by temperature. If this activity were repeated at a higher temperature, the food coloring would spread more rapidly. At a lower temperature, it would spread more slowly.

↑ Add a few drops of food coloring to the water. Make sure the water has been left to settle for a few hours before adding the coloring.

↑ Leave the glass for about 30 minutes. When you come back, you should see that the food coloring has spread through the water.

forces that determine whether a substance is a solid, liquid, or gas.

External Forces

Intermolecular forces attract molecules to one another. Inter means "between" or "among." Compared with intramolecular forces, intermolecular forces are weak. In fact, intermolecular forces are typically only about 15 percent of the strength of intramolecular forces. There are three main types of intermolecular forces. These are the dipole–dipole forces, the London dispersion forces, and hydrogen bonding forces. All of these attractions involve partial electric charges. The charges result from the arrangement of electrons and nuclei in the molecule. Sometimes the arrangement of electrons leaves the nucleus partially exposed, resulting in a small positive charge. At the same time, the electrons are bunched together, producing a small negative charge. It is the attraction between these charges that attracts molecules to one another.

When a substance boils, the particles in the substance have enough kinetic energy to overcome the intermolecular forces. Boiling is a process by which particles gain enough

IONIC AND COVALENT BONDS

Two of the strongest intramolecular forces are the ionic and covalent bonds that bind atoms together. Ionic bonds occur when one atom gives one or more electrons to an atom that is trying to fill its outer shell. Covalent bonds are shared between two atoms that both have nearly full shells.

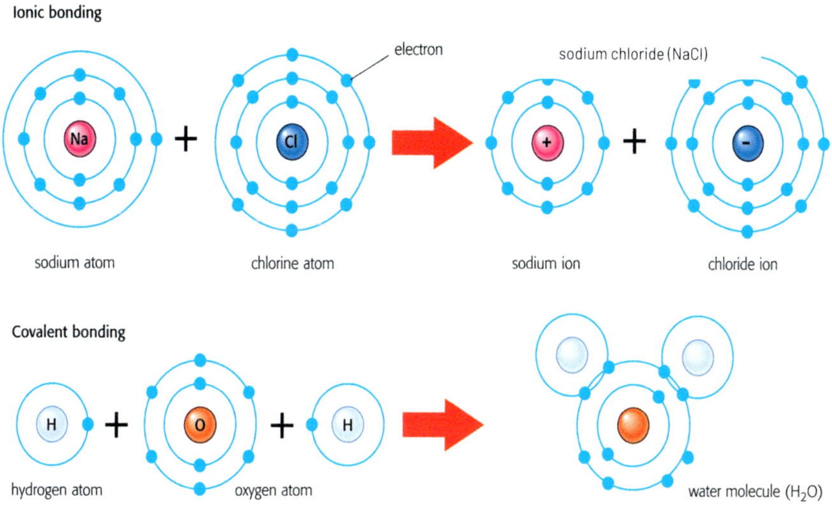

energy to jump out of a liquid phase and become a gas. The kinetic energy to make this possible comes from the heat applied to the liquid. Substances with higher boiling points have stronger intermolecular forces than substances with lower boiling points.

KEY TERMS

Intermolecular bond: Weak bond between one molecule and another.
Intramolecular bond: Strong bond between atoms in a molecule.

Hydrogen Bonds

Hydrogen bonds are a stronger form of intermolecular bond. Water molecules are attracted to one another by these bonds. Water molecules have a neutral charge overall—their number of electrons balances their number of protons. However, water molecules have partial charges at specific locations on the molecule that are strongly attracted to the opposite charge on another water molecule. As a result, water molecules need a bigger input of energy to provide them with enough kinetic energy to overcome the force of the hydrogen bonds. Water therefore has an unusually high

EXPERIMENTING WITH ICE

Materials: glass, water, ice

When ice is added to a glass of water, it raises the water level in the glass. Many people think that when ice melts, it will raise the water level even more because there is ice sticking out of the water. This is not the case. Try it for yourself and see what happens. Put a few cubes of ice into a glass and place it on a flat surface. Fill the glass with water up to the rim. Some of the ice cubes will be sticking out above the rim of the glass. Watch as the ice melts. Even when it has all melted, none of the water will have spilled over the edge because there is still the same mass of water in the glass and the liquid occupies less volume than the solid.

HYDROGEN BONDS

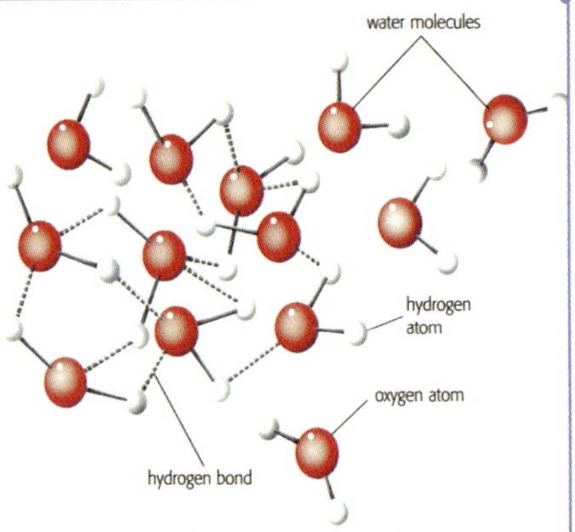

Water molecules are attracted to one another by weak forces called hydrogen bonds. It is this type of bonding that keeps water liquid at room temperature.

boiling point. Water's high boiling point is not its only unusual property. Ice is one of the few solid phases that floats in its own liquid phase. Ice floats in water because when it becomes a solid, the hydrogen bonds hold the water molecules apart rather than allowing them to get closer together, as in other solids. This gives ice a

Gallium is a rare metal element that is solid at room temperature, but heat energy from the palm of your hand is enough to melt it. The bonds between the atoms in solid gallium are not very strong. The heat energy from your palm makes the atoms vibrate until the bonds break, and the solid becomes a liquid.

PLASMA: THE FOURTH STATE

Plasma is considered to be a fourth state of matter. Plasmas consist of freely moving charged particles, such as electrons, and particles called ions, which are atoms that have lost or gained one or more electrons.

Plasmas are formed when the electrons are stripped away from atoms. Stripping electrons from atoms requires a lot of energy. Therefore, the particles in plasmas have very high energy. Such high energies give plasmas unique properties that make them distinct from solids, liquids, and gases. Examples of plasmas include the sun, lightning, the northern lights, fluorescent lights, and flames. Plasmas are actually the most common form of matter, making up 99 percent of the visible universe and probably much of that which we cannot see.

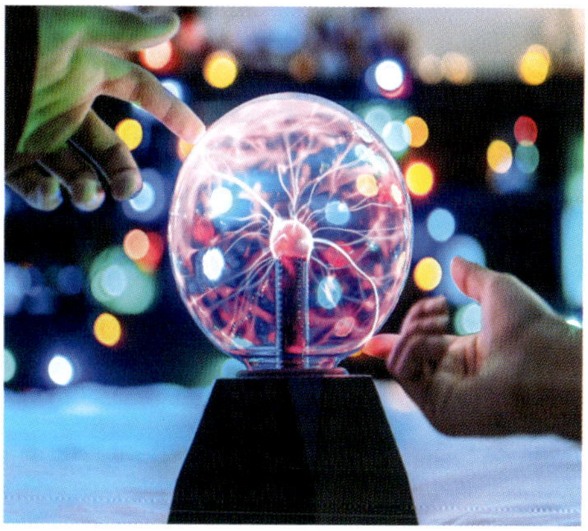

↑ Plasma globes are a fun way of seeing the effect of a plasma. These glass globes are filled with a gas at low pressure. At the center is a metal ball that is charged with electricity. When there is enough electricity on the metal ball, sparks travel between the ball and the glass wall. The heat from the sparks strips electrons off the gas atoms, turning the gas into a plasma and causing it to emit light.

lower density than water, so it floats. Ice does not have a much lower density than water, so only a small portion of ice sticks out of the water, as seen in icebergs.

Changing States of Matter

When heat is added to a solid, its atoms vibrate more rapidly and its temperature increases. At a certain temperature, a solid will begin to melt. As more energy is added to the solid, its temperature does not increase, but more of the solid melts. Eventually all of the solid will have melted and become a liquid—it will have changed state from solid to liquid. Now if more energy is added, the temperature of the liquid will increase. Similarly, at a certain temperature, the liquid will begin to turn into a gas. As more energy is added to the liquid, its temperature does not increase, but more of the liquid becomes a gas. Eventually all of the liquid will turn into a gas. Now if more energy is added, the temperature of the gas will increase. Energy is either used to increase the temperature of a substance or to change its state.

CHAPTER 2

Gases and Their Properties

Gases have no fixed shape or volume. They also have a lower density than other states of matter. If gases are compressed, the particles exert a force called pressure.

Earth is surrounded by a layer of mixed gases that we call the atmosphere. In this photograph, the atmosphere is visible as a hazy blue ring around the planet. The way these gases react to the warmth of the sun as they pass over land or sea makes them contract or expand. The resulting changes in pressure create our weather systems.

Solids and liquids are easy to see, but gases are usually invisible. Scientists began to study gases more than 300 years ago. The first gas they studied was air. When scientists first started studying air, they did not know that it is composed of many different gases. One of their most surprising discoveries was that even though air is a mixture of gases, it still behaves the same way as a pure gas. In fact, gases all behave in a similar manner regardless of whether they are composed of single atoms, paired atoms, or molecules of many types of atoms.

Because of this common behavior, the rules applying to any one gas also apply to all other types. When gases

This huge balloon floats because it is filled with helium gas. Helium atoms have less mass per unit of volume than most other gases. That makes them lighter than the surrounding air, so the balloon floats upward.

are compared with each other, they are compared at the same temperature and pressure. The standard used to compare gases is called Standard Temperature and Pressure, or STP. In STP, temperature is measured using the Celsius scale or the Kelvin scale.

Pressure is measured in units called atmospheres. STP is defined as 0°C (or 273K, –32°F) and 1 atmosphere of pressure. Scientists use the Kelvin scale when doing calculations involving gases and temperatures. Zero on the Kelvin scale is the coldest temperature theoretically possible in the universe (–273°C; –459°F). Temperatures on the Kelvin scale are always positive. Using the Kelvin scale simplifies any calculations.

Chemists often compare gases by using a unit called a mole. A mole of any substance contains 602,213,670,000,000,000,000,000 (6.022 x 10^{23}) atoms or molecules. At STP, 1 mole of any gas has a volume of 3 cubic feet (22.4 L).

GAS MOLECULES

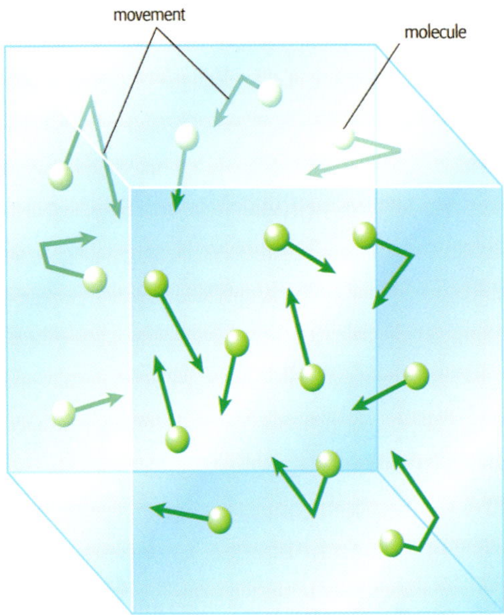

Molecules of gas inside a container will move through the space available until the particles are all evenly distributed.

Physical Properties

All gases share a set of physical properties. The following six properties are common to all gases:

1. All gases have mass.

Mass is a measure of the amount of matter something contains. A helium-filled balloon has mass, but it floats because its mass is less than that of the gases in the surrounding air.

2. Gases are easily compressed.

Scuba tanks and car tires are filled with compressed air. Solids and liquids are not easily compressed.

Molecules of one gas introduced into another gas will move by random collisions until the introduced gas is evenly spread out. This process is termed diffusion.

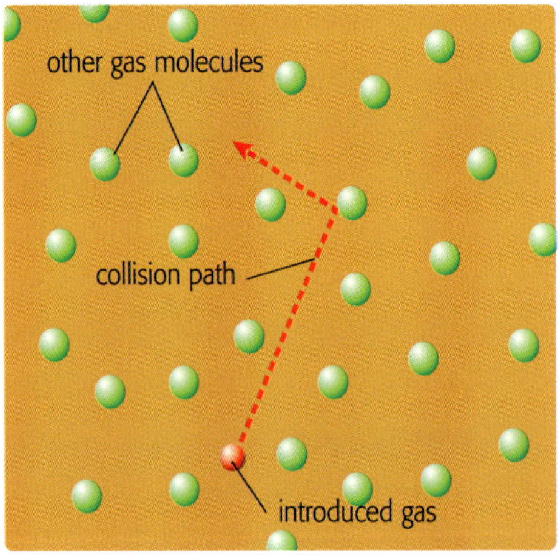

EXPERIMENT WITH BUBBLES

Materials: dish soap, water, baking soda, vinegar, bubble wand, small bowl, small bottle with lid, rubber tubing

1. Make a hole in the lid of the bottle just big enough to fit the rubber tubing into it.

2. Mix a small amount of dish soap with water in the bowl.

3. Dip the bubble wand into the soapy water, then wave the wand in the air. The bubbles should float.

4. Add a small amount of baking soda, water, and vinegar to the bottle. Put the lid on. This reaction produces carbon dioxide.

5. Dip the bubble wand into the soapy water and hold it close to the end of the rubber tubing. There should be enough carbon dioxide coming out of the tube to blow bubbles of carbon dioxide. They will drop to the ground. That is because carbon dioxide is heavier than air.

3. Gases fill the available space.

In a container, gases spread out until they are evenly distributed. When you blow up a balloon, air is distributed throughout the balloon. The air will not concentrate in any one part of the balloon.

4. Different gases move through each other easily.

The movement of one gas through another is called diffusion. Diffusion occurs because of the random motion of the gas particles colliding with each other. Eventually the gas particles become evenly spread out. Diffusion explains why air is a mixture of gases.

5. Gases exert pressure.

The air in car tires is under pressure. You may have also experienced a pressure change in a car, plane, or elevator. When going up rapidly, your ears may pop. That happens because the ears need to maintain a constant pressure to protect your eardrums.

6. The pressure of a gas depends on its temperature.

When the temperature is high, gas pressure increases. When the temperature is low, the pressure decreases. That happens with car tires. In places with very hot summers, tires can become dangerously overinflated.

DIFFUSION AND EFFUSION

Sometimes gas particles are so small that they pass through the space between molecules a single particle at a time. This process is related to diffusion, but it is called effusion. These pictures illustrate how effusion affects balloons filled with different gases.

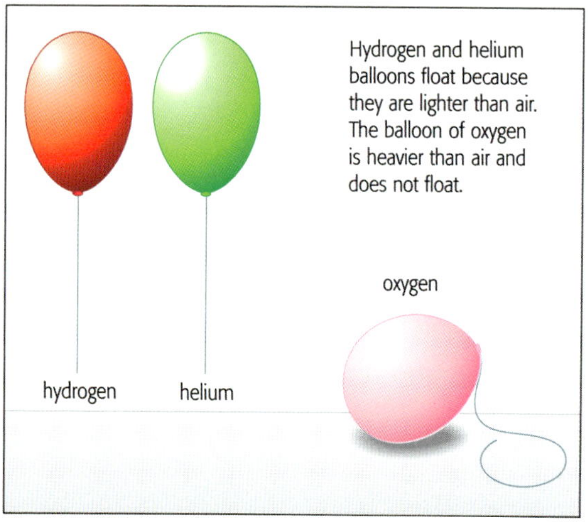

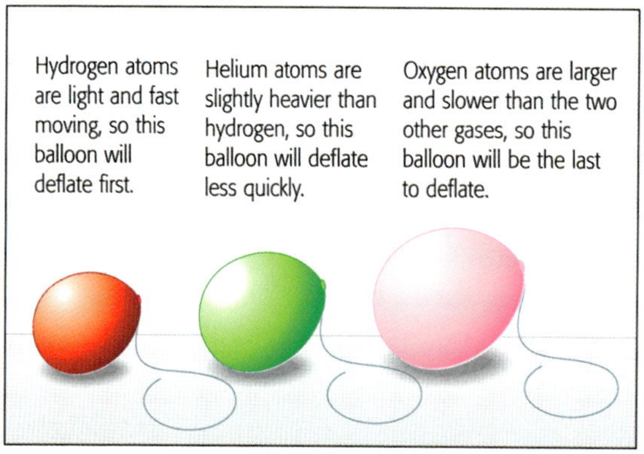

↑ The rate at which a gas can escape by effusion depends on its molecular mass and how fast the molecules are moving. Lighter and faster-moving gases will effuse more quickly than slow, heavy ones.

In places with cold winters, the opposite happens: Tires can deflate and become soft in cold weather.

These six properties of gas are all explained by the kinetic molecular theory. Using this theory, scientists can construct a model that explains each of these behaviors for any gas.

Kinetic Theory

All six properties of gas can be explained by the kinetic theory. Gas particles have higher kinetic energy than particles in solids or liquids, and gas particles are always colliding with each other. One way to imagine a container of gas is to think of a large jar filled with small rubber balls. As you shake the jar, the rubber balls bounce off each other and the walls of the jar. However, gas particles have their own kinetic energy, so the container does not need to be shaken.

These collisions of gas particles are described as elastic collisions. An elastic collision means that no energy is lost in the collision. Rubber balls do not have elastic collisions. When

PRESSURES OF DIVING

You cannot feel it, but the atmosphere is pressing down on your body all the time. Water also exerts pressure. The deeper you go, the greater the pressure. At the surface, pressure is defined as 1 atmosphere. For every 33 feet (10 m) in depth, a diver is exposed to another atmosphere of pressure. This pressure is a concern for divers because it forces nitrogen gas in their blood to dissolve. If divers rise to the surface too quickly, the sudden release of pressure forms nitrogen bubbles in their blood, causing pain and sometimes death.

Pressurized chambers used by divers bring their blood gases slowly back to normal levels. This process can take several hours.

you drop a rubber ball, it bounces, but each bounce becomes lower than the previous bounce because some of the energy is transferred to the surface it is bouncing on. If a rubber ball could have a perfectly elastic bounce, it would continue bouncing back to exactly the same height.

Because gas particles have kinetic energy, they strike the walls of their container, which creates pressure. One of the properties of gases is that as temperature increases, pressure increases. That is explained by the fact that at higher temperatures, the gas particles are moving faster, so there are more collisions with the wall of the container. The kinetic theory of gases can be

KEY TERMS

Compress: To reduce in size or volume by squeezing or exerting pressure.
Gas: A substance, such as air, that spreads out to fill the available space.
Mole: The amount of any substance that contains the same number of atoms or molecules as 12 grams of carbon. This number is called Avogadro's number and equals 6.022×10^{23}, which written out equals 602,213,670,000,000,000,000,000.
Pressure: The force produced by pressing on something.
Temperature: A measure of the hotness or coldness of a substance.
Volume: The space that a solid, liquid, or gas occupies.

summarized in four statements:

1. A gas consists of particles in constant random motion.

2. Gas particles influence each other only by collision; they exert no other forces on each other.

3. All collisions between gas particles are perfectly elastic; all kinetic energy is conserved—the total amount of kinetic energy in the gas remains the same.

4. The volume occupied by the particles of a gas is very small; the vast majority of a gas's volume is empty space through which the gas molecules are moving.

COMPRESSION

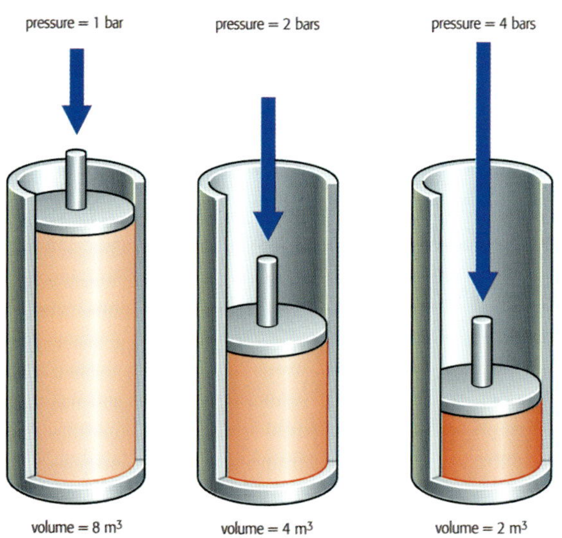

Robert Boyle's experiment on compressing gas trapped in a piston showed that when the pressure on a gas is increased, its volume decreases. A bar is a metric unit of pressure. 1 bar = just under the average atmospheric pressure on Earth at sea level.

EXPERIMENTING WITH BALLOONS

Materials: balloon, freezer

1. Blow up a balloon. Measure the circumference.

2. Place the balloon in the freezer for about 30 minutes.

3. Remove the balloon from the freezer. How does the size of the balloon compare with its size when it was placed in the freezer?

What do you think will happen as the balloon warms up? Watch and find out. The balloon changes size because the molecules slow down as the temperature decreases and speed up as the temperature increases.

Measuring a Gas

Four variables are used to describe a gas. These variables are also used to predict how a gas will behave when conditions are changed. The four variables are volume, temperature, pressure, and the number of gas molecules.

The amount of gas (n) is the quantity of gas expressed in moles. The amount of gas in the sample being measured is found by dividing the mass (in grams) of the gas by the mass of one mole of the gas (in grams per mole).

The volume (V) of a gas is the size of the container. The volume of gases is usually measured in liters (L).

The temperature (T) is usually measured with a thermometer. Scientists measure temperature in degrees Celsius (°C). Calculations involving gases use the Kelvin (K) scale to measure temperature. Adding 273 to the temperature in degrees Celsius gives the temperature in Kelvin.

The pressure (P) is the measure of the number of collisions by particles with the wall of the container. Because the particles strike all surfaces of the container, the pressure is the outward force of the particles pushing against the interior surface of the container.

The Gas Laws

When scientists first started studying gases, they found that all gases behave similarly when certain conditions change. These observations eventually led to a number of scientific laws that describe the behavior of gases. These scientific laws are called the gas laws. The gas laws can be expressed mathematically using the variables of quantity of gas, volume, temperature, and pressure.

DEMONSTRATION

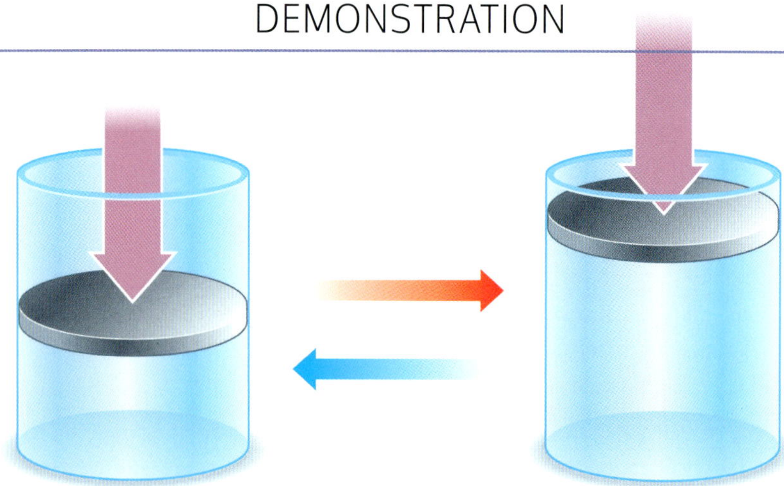

Jacques Charles's experiment with a movable piston demonstrated how heating a gas changes its volume. At room temperature, the piston is at one level.

When heat is applied to the container, the gas molecules become more energetic and start to exert pressure on the piston, forcing it upward. When the heat is removed, the piston sinks as the gas loses energy and cools.

Jacques Charles was a French physicist who studied gases. From his work on hydrogen, oxygen, and nitrogen, he discovered that a gas will expand by $^1/_{273}$ of its volume at 0°C for every degree rise in temperature. Charles was the first person to go up in a hydrogen-filled balloon, reaching nearly 10,000 feet (3,000 m) on one of his later flights.

Boyle's Law

In the seventeenth century, an English chemist and physicist named Robert Boyle (1627–1691) noticed that air could be compressed. He performed a series of experiments with air sealed in a tube. By increasing or decreasing the pressure, he found that the volume changed. His experiments showed there was a mathematical relationship between the pressure and volume. He expressed this relationship with the following equation:

$$P_1V_1 = P_2V_2$$

The equation tells us that the initial pressure of the gas (P_1) multiplied by its initial volume (V_1) is equal to the final pressure of the gas (P_2) multiplied by its final volume (V_2).

According to this equation, if pressure increases, volume decreases. In turn, if pressure decreases, the volume increases. Because the values change in opposite directions, this is called an inverse relationship.

Hot air balloons rise because as the air inside is heated, the molecules gain energy and move farther apart, thus increasing the volume of the air inside the balloon.

Charles's Law

The eighteenth-century French chemist, physicist, and aeronaut Jacques Charles (1746–1823) was also interested in gases. His work centered on the relationship between temperature and volume of a gas. He designed an experimental device that trapped a gas with a movable piston. He could heat or cool the container and measure how much the piston moved as the temperature changed. By finding how much the piston moved, he could calculate the change in the volume of the gas at the different temperatures. He expressed this relationship with the following equation:

$$V_1/T_1 = V_2/T_2$$

This equation tells us that the initial volume (V_1) divided by the initial temperature (T_1) is equal to the final volume (V_2) divided by the final temperature (T_2).

The higher you climb above sea level, the lower the atmospheric pressure becomes. At the top of Mount Everest, the atmosphere is very thin. Mountaineers carry oxygen supplies with them because there are not enough oxygen molecules at this level. The atmospheric pressure is too low to make the air flow easily into their lungs.

According to the equation $V_1/T_1 = V_2/T_2$, if the temperature increases, the volume also increases. Conversely, if the temperature decreases, the volume also decreases. Because the values change in the same direction, this is called a direct relationship. In the shrinking balloon activity, this relationship is shown by comparing the balloon before and after it is placed in the freezer compartment.

Avogadro's Law

In the early nineteenth century, the Italian chemist Amedeo Avogadro (1776–1856) suggested a simple yet profound relationship between the number of particles of a gas and its volume. This relationship states that equal volumes of gases at the same temperature and pressure contain an equal number of particles.

Later, scientists proved that Avogadro's hypothesis was correct. Experiments have shown that 1 mole of any gas at STP occupies 22.4 liters. Avogadro's law is expressed with the following mathematical equation:

$$V_1/n_1 = V_2/n_2$$

This equation shows that the initial volume of a gas (V_1) divided by the initial number of moles (n_1) is equal to the final volume of the gas (V_2) divided by the final number of moles (n_2). Put more simply, if the volume of a gas increases, the number of moles increases proportionally. This is true only if the temperature and pressure of the gas remain the same throughout the experiment. The equation shows a direct relationship because as volume increases, the number of moles increases, too.

The Ideal Gas Law

The three gas laws all relate to certain variables that describe gases. These gas

GAS LAWS

Law	Statement	Equation	Constants
Boyle's law	P is inversely proportional to V	$P_1V_1 = P_2V_2$	Temperature and number of moles
Charles's law	V is directly proportional to T	$V_1/T_1 = V_2/T_2$	Pressure and number of moles
Avogadro's law	V is directly proportional to n	$V_1/n_1 = V_2/n_2$	Pressure and temperature

P = Pressure V = Volume T = Temperature n = Number of moles

laws can be combined in one equation called the ideal gas law. This combines the proportionalities expressed in each equation. When combined, the ideal gas law is stated as:

$$PV = nRT$$

Four of these quantities have been described in detail already. The only new one is the constant R. The constant R is called the gas constant. The value of the gas constant is 8.314 $Jmol^{-1}K^{-1}$. The units in this constant are energy in joules (J) per mole (mol^{-1}) per degree Kelvin (K^{-1}). This constant represents the conditions of a gas at STP.

Chemists call this the ideal gas law because it describes the behavior of an ideal gas in terms of pressure, volume, temperature, and moles. An ideal gas to a chemist is one described by the kinetic theory. While there is really no such thing as an ideal gas, it does describe the behavior of real gases under conditions near STP. At very low temperatures, gases do not behave as ideal gases.

Measuring Gas Pressure

Gas pressure is measured in atmospheres. The instrument used to measure air pressure is the barometer. Air pressure is caused by the pull of gravity on the gases in the atmosphere.

Air pressure varies with changes in the weather. Air pressure also changes with elevation. As elevation increases, air pressure decreases. The air pressure decreases about 1 inch of mercury for every 1,000-foot rise, or 1 millibar for each 8-meter rise. In a commercial airline jet, when cruising at 35,000 feet (10,600 m), the air pressure outside the plane is only $^1/_{20}$ of the pressure at sea level.

CHAPTER 3

Liquids and Their Properties

Liquids have no shape of their own. They cannot be squashed. They can be thick or thin. Some liquids, such as water, have a number of different properties. Water is colorless, tasteless, odorless, and vital to life on Earth.

Liquids take the shape of whatever container they are put in. However, the volume of the liquid does not change with the size or shape of the container.

Liquids have a definite volume, unlike gases, but they can change shape. In gases, the particles are far enough apart and have enough kinetic energy to change volume. In liquids, the particles are much closer together and they have forces that attract the particles to each other.

Even though the particles are close together and are attracted to each other, they have enough kinetic energy to slide past each other. The ability to move in this way allows a liquid to take the shape of its container.

↑ The seas are the largest bodies of liquid on the planet. They have no shape of their own; they mold themselves to the shapes of the solid land barriers that confine them.

Substances that are liquids at room temperature and a pressure of 1 atmosphere are made of molecules. These molecules have varying intermolecular forces that affect how close the molecules are to each other and how they interact. The strength of the intermolecular forces also affects certain physical properties of the liquid.

Physical Properties

If you have ever tried to pour honey, you know that it pours very slowly compared to water. Honey is very thick. The term used to describe how a liquid pours is viscosity. Viscosity is defined as a liquid's resistance to flow. Honey has a high viscosity and water has a low viscosity. So, while water flows freely, honey does not. The intermolecular forces in a liquid cause viscosity. If the intermolecular forces are strong, the molecules do not slide past each other easily and the viscosity is high.

Viscosity is affected by temperature. At higher temperatures, the molecules have more energy. Because they have more energy, they are able to overcome some of the intermolecular forces and move more easily. This reduces viscosity. At low temperatures, viscosity increases because the molecules have less energy.

Water has hydrogen bonds that act as strong intermolecular forces. Even though water pours more easily than honey, it is still fairly viscous for its molecular size. By comparison, rubbing alcohol has a low viscosity. If you pour equal amounts of water and rubbing alcohol onto a surface, the rubbing alcohol spreads more quickly.

↑ Honey is a sticky liquid with a high viscosity. This is a measure of a fluid's resistance to flow. It is viscosity that makes honey slow to flow off a surface.

Another property of liquids is called surface tension. You may have seen an insect called a water strider skate on the surface of water. The water strider is held up by the surface tension of the water. Uneven forces cause surface tension at the surface of a liquid. The uneven forces cause the surface of the liquid to act like a film. Water has a rather high surface tension. To demonstrate the strength of surface tension, perform the needle experiment on page 30 and float a needle on water using surface tension.

Surface tension explains why water beads up on a surface. Scattered raindrops on a window have a circular shape. That is caused by the surface tension of the water. The water drops take on a circular shape as this minimizes the surface area.

Surface tension is related to viscosity. Liquids with a high viscosity have a high surface tension. A drop of honey on a plate will hold its circular shape. If you place a drop of rubbing alcohol on a plate, however, it will spread out over a large area. The rubbing alcohol has a low surface tension because the intermolecular forces between molecules are low.

Like viscosity, surface tension is affected by temperature. At a lower temperature, the surface tension is greater because molecules have less kinetic energy, so it is more difficult for them to overcome the intermolecular forces. At a higher temperature, the molecules have more kinetic energy, so they create less surface tension.

These seeds are floating on the surface of a pond rather than sinking. That happens because water has a high surface tension, which acts like a film across the surface. The seeds are not heavy enough to overcome the forces that are supporting the top layers of the water molecules, so they cannot sink.

MOTOR OIL

Motor oil is available in various viscosities. You may have heard of 30-weight or 40-weight motor oil. The term "weight" refers to the viscosity. The higher the weight, the higher the viscosity. Motor oil is exposed to high temperatures in an engine, especially when it is warm outside. It is important to choose a motor oil with the proper viscosity for the weather, to prevent wear and tear on the engine.

Some oils are described as being multiweight oils. Chemicals called polymers are added to the oil. They control how the viscosity changes when heated. Multiweight oils are better for car engines in variable climates because they maintain the proper viscosity over a wide range of temperatures.

Adding another substance to the liquid may also reduce surface tension. Soap is used to reduce the surface tension of water. If you repeat the needle experiment on page 30, you can add a drop of dish soap to the bowl of water and the needle will sink immediately. Sometimes it is useful to reduce the surface tension of a liquid. Water beads up on a car when it is wet. At car washes, chemicals are added to the rinse water to lower the surface tension of the water. This causes the water droplets to spread out rather than bead up, so the water rinses the detergent away more quickly.

↑ Jets of water at a car wash are mixed with chemicals that make water run off the car's surface more quickly.

Water for Life

Water is the most common liquid on Earth. It is in the oceans, in the atmosphere, and in rivers, lakes, and glaciers. All living organisms need water, and water is an

SURFACE TENSION

The surface tension of a liquid is a result of the forces between molecules. In the body of the liquid, molecules are surrounded on all sides, so the forces they exert are even in all directions. On the surface, the molecules have no other liquid molecules above them, so the horizontal forces between their nearest neighbors become stronger. This allows them to form a firm surface layer.

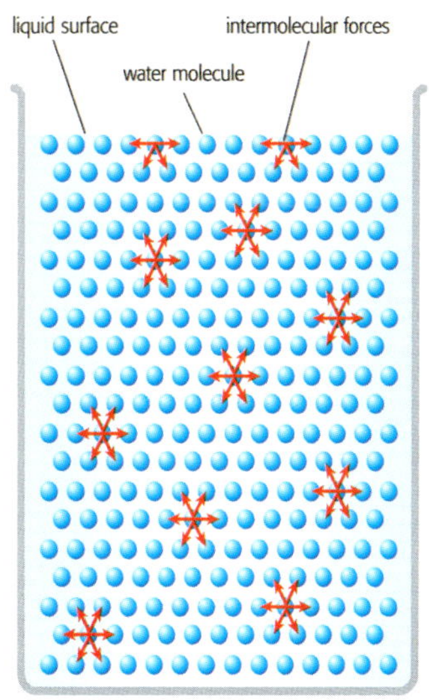

NEEDLE EXPERIMENT

Materials: sewing needle, water, bowl, tweezers

1. Fill the bowl with water.

2. Hold the needle horizontally with the tweezers.

3. Slowly lower the needle to the surface of the water.

4. When the needle is horizontal with and touching the water's surface, release the needle. The needle should float on the surface of the water. It may take several tries before you get the needle to float. The needle floats because water has a very high surface tension and is able to support the mass of the needle.

important part of a body. In fact, the human body is about 60 percent water. Even though water is common on Earth, it has many special and unusual properties.

The solid form of water floats in the liquid form. This rare property is shared by very few substances. This property is important in nature. When a lake freezes over, the ice blanket insulates the water below from the freezing temperatures above. This allows plants and animals in the water to survive.

Water also has a high boiling point for a compound with its molecular size. Other compounds with a similar size such as ammonia (NH_3), hydrofluoric acid (HF), and hydrogen sulfide (H_2S) are all gases at room temperature.

Water absorbs a large amount of heat for its volume. The large heat capacity of water helps moderate the overall temperature of Earth. It resists huge temperature changes between day and night by absorbing and releasing heat.

Water turns into a gas only at very high temperatures. It takes considerable energy to turn water from a liquid to a gas.

The high surface tension of water leads to a phenomenon called capillary action. Because of the unequal forces at the surface of water, water will rise in a narrow tube. Capillary action is responsible in part for water being carried up from a tree's roots to its leaves.

Water is also very good at dissolving other substances. Because it is so good at this, it is often called the universal solvent. A solvent is a liquid that dissolves another substance to form a solution.

Converting Liquid to Gas

When enough heat is added to a liquid, it begins to boil and turn into a gas. This temperature is called the boiling point. Adding heat to a liquid gives the molecules in the liquid more kinetic energy. When they get enough kinetic energy, they can escape the intermolecular forces of the liquid and become a gas. The process of a liquid changing into a gas is also called vaporization. Vaporization describes boiling and it also describes evaporation. If you have ever left a glass of water sitting out for a long period, you may have noticed the volume decrease over time. Some of the water molecules have escaped from the liquid and become gas. The term for this is evaporation. When a liquid evaporates, it changes to a gas without boiling. Temperature is a measure of the average kinetic energy. In reality, some molecules have more energy than average and others have less. Some of the molecules

↑ Water reaches the leaves at the top of a tree by capillary action. It can be seen in the demonstration above. The surface tension and density of a liquid determines how far up a piece of paper the liquid will go. Trees have long, narrow tubes in their stems that pull water up.

FALLING RAINDROPS

People often describe raindrops as teardrop-shaped. However, when raindrops fall from the sky, they are not shaped like that. Water has a high surface tension, and that tends to pull all the molecules together when in a drop. This makes a water drop spherical in shape because all the surface forces are equal in a sphere. As a raindrop falls, its bottom surface flattens slightly as a result of air resistance, but the top of the raindrop remains well rounded.

This high-speed photograph of a water droplet shows that it is not shaped like a teardrop but is almost spherical.

with more kinetic energy have enough energy to overcome intermolecular forces and escape the liquid to become a gas. As temperature increases, evaporation increases because more molecules have enough energy to escape the liquid.

If you place some water in a container and pump out the excess air, the liquid will evaporate until the pressure of the liquid and its vapor are in equilibrium. The pressure of the vapor at this point is called the liquid's vapor pressure. At the same time as some water molecules evaporate, some of the molecules in the vapor condense or return to the liquid. In equilibrium, the rate of evaporation and the rate of condensation are equal.

All liquids create a vapor. In liquids with low intermolecular forces, evaporation does not require as much energy. You have already learned that rubbing alcohol has a low viscosity and low surface tension because the intermolecular forces are weak. Alcohol also evaporates much more quickly than water because the molecules do not need as much energy to escape the liquid.

VAPOR EXPERIMENT

Materials: large, strong jar; measuring cup; water; floating candle; rubber glove

Water vapor is a colorless gas. However, if it cools quickly, it can form tiny droplets that appear white as they scatter light. That is what happens in the water vapor trails you see behind jets.

1. Pour about ¼ cup of water into the jar.

2. Turn the rubber glove inside out. Place a floating candle inside the jar and ask an adult to light it. After a few seconds, blow it out and quickly stretch the glove completely over the mouth of the jar.

3. Put your hand inside the glove and push your hand into the jar. Take care not to touch the candle—it may still be hot.

4. Carefully bend your fingers into a fist and pull up while holding the jar steady. You should see a cloud form in the jar. The cloud will disappear when you stop pulling up. The cloud forms because the change in pressure causes some of the water vapor to condense (change back to a liquid) and become visible.

FREEZE-DRYING FOOD

A process called freeze-drying preserves many foods. Freeze-drying removes all the water from a food. That allows the food to be stored for long periods of time at room temperature. When it is time to eat, hot water is added to the food. The food absorbs the water and is then ready to eat. Freeze-drying is useful because many of the flavors and smells are retained.

Freeze-drying uses the pressure of water vapor to work. The food is first frozen and then exposed to a low temperature and pressure so the frozen water in the food becomes a gas without becoming liquid again. The gas escapes the food. The food is then sealed to prevent moisture from reaching it. The food can be stored for later use. Backpackers find this especially useful because freeze-drying makes the food lighter to carry.

Boiling Liquid

When you heat a pan of water, tiny bubbles form on the bottom of the pan, which reaches boiling point first. These bubbles are water vapor. As more heat is added, more of the water reaches boiling point and the bubbles become larger. Soon, the bubbles are rising to the surface quickly and in great number. When you see this happen, you know the water is boiling. Sometimes the small bubbles appear even before the bottom of the pan has reached the boiling point. These are air bubbles resulting from air that was dissolved in the water, since the solubility of air in water goes down as the temperature increases.

If you try to boil an egg at a high elevation, such as at the top of a mountain, it takes longer to boil than it does at sea level. This is because the atmospheric pressure is lower at high altitude. Water boils when the vapor pressure is equal

PHASE DIAGRAM: WATER

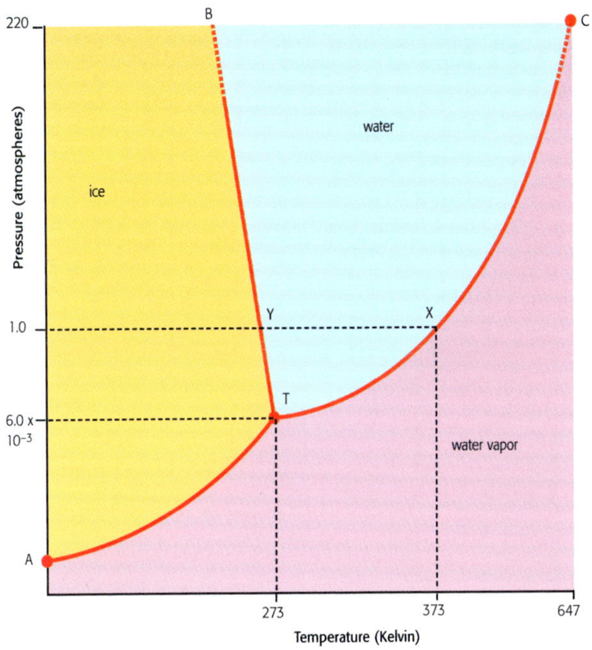

The phase diagram for water shows the physical state in which water occurs at any given temperature and pressure. Point T is called the triple point. At this point, water can exist in all three phases—solid, liquid, and gas—at the same time. Point X is the boiling point, and point Y is the freezing point at standard conditions. Point C is the critical point. The curve BT marks the boundary between ice and water; CT is the boundary between water and vapor; and AT is the boundary between ice and vapor. Along these boundaries, the two phases are said to be in equilibrium.

to the atmospheric pressure. At high altitude, the atmospheric pressure is lower, so the temperature at which water boils is also lower. In fact, if you lower the pressure enough, water will boil at room temperature.

Critical Point

If the temperature and pressure of a liquid are both increased, the vapor becomes more dense while the liquid becomes less dense. The point at which the density of vapor and liquid become equal is called the critical point. Above this temperature, vapor cannot be turned into a liquid, even under high pressure.

A phase diagram shows that states of matter are affected by temperature and pressure. The effects on water in a closed container were discussed previously. When water reaches the vapor pressure, the rates of evaporation and condensation are the same. The phase diagram above shows the vapor pressure as a line. Along this boundary, water can exist as both a liquid and a gas at the same time.

CHAPTER 4

Solutions and Mixtures

A solution is a mixture where one substance, the solute, is dissolved in another substance, the solvent. The particles of a solution are bonded, evenly distributed, and hard to separate. A mixture is a combination of two or more substances that are not chemically bonded, so they can be physically separated.

There are two basic types of mixtures: homogeneous and heterogeneous. In a homogeneous mixture, the substances included are mixed evenly so you cannot tell one from another. In a heterogeneous mixture, all the ingredients are still identifiable, and they can be separated from each other relatively easily. Seawater is a homogeneous mixture. It is not possible to see the water, salts, and other things mixed into it. A bowl of noodle soup is a heterogeneous mixture. You can see the broth, noodles, and other ingredients.

A solution is the most common type of homogeneous mixture. This is a mixture that is in a single physical state. The most familiar solutions, such as seawater or soda, are liquids. Solutions can also be gases or solids. The air is a solution of gases, while bronze is a solid solution.

← A tablet dissolves in water. As it does so, the tablet breaks up into its smallest units and spreads throughout the water.

Oil poured into a bowl of water forms a layer at the top. Oil and water will not mix. If the two liquids are left to stand, they will always separate into layers, with the water at the bottom.

Solution Properties

To have a solution, there must be one or more substances dissolved into another substance. The substance that is dissolved is called a solute. The substance that the solute is dissolved into is called the solvent. For example, if you add a spoonful of table salt to a glass of water, you make a solution. The table salt dissolves in the water, so the salt is the solute. The water is the solvent.

Not every substance will dissolve in every other substance. You may have heard people say that oil and water do not mix. You can demonstrate this by adding oil to water. If a solute does not dissolve in solvent, it is called insoluble. If a solute does dissolve in a solvent, it is described as soluble.

KEY TERMS

Heterogenous mixture: A mixture in which ingredients are not spread evenly.
Homogeneous mixture: A mixture in which substances are spread out and distributed evenly.
Insoluble: When a substance will not dissolve in another substance.
Soluble: When a substance can dissolve in another substance.
Solute: A substance that is dissolved to form a solution.
Solution: A homogeneous mixture where substances are in the same physical state.
Solvent: A substance in which a solute is dissolved.

Solution Types

Most people think of solutions as being liquids, but that does not have to be the case. Solutions can be any combination of solutes and solvents in different states. Solid solutions generally involve at least one metal. For example, sterling silver has a small amount of copper mixed into it. The silver is the solvent and the copper is the solute. Gold used for jewelry also has copper dissolved in it, and steel is made by dissolving a small amount of carbon in iron. Solid solutions that include metals are called alloys. Alloys are made by mixing the metals while they are melted into liquids.

Solutions of gases are homogeneous mixtures of two or more gases. An example of a gaseous solution is air. Air is composed of mainly oxygen and nitrogen. Most of it—78 percent—is nitrogen, so that is the solvent. Oxygen makes up 21 percent of the air, so it is the main solute. Air also contains several other gas solutes, including argon and carbon dioxide.

Liquid solutions must have a liquid solvent, but they can involve a solid, liquid, or gas as a solute. For example, water in a river has oxygen dissolved in it. Fish and many other underwater creatures depend on this oxygen for their survival. Solids can form solutions with liquids, too. For example, sugar will dissolve in hot water.

Liquids that dissolve liquids are less common. One example is the antifreeze added to the water in a car's radiator. The water dissolves in the antifreeze, which prevents the water from freezing.

Liquids that mix easily, like antifreeze and water, are said to be miscible. Other liquids, such as oil and water, do not mix at all. Liquids that do not mix are described as immiscible.

Dissolving Substances

Water is sometimes called the universal solvent because it can dissolve so many different substances. The solutions water forms are described as aqueous solutions. The term "aqueous" comes from *aqua*, the Latin word for "water." A solute that dissolves in water either forms ions or molecules. An ion is an atom that has lost or gained one or more electrons. As a result, the ion has a charge. An ion that has lost electrons has a positive charge, while one that has gained an electron is negatively charged. A molecule is a collection of two or more atoms connected by chemical bonds. Molecules do not have a charge.

Ions are attracted to other ions that have an opposite charge. They are repelled by ions with the same charge. The attraction makes ions combine to form compounds. Compounds are substances that contain the atoms of two or more elements joined together by chemical bonds. An ionic compound always contains both positive and negative ions. When these compounds dissolve in water, the ions separate.

Table salt, or sodium chloride, is an example of an ionic compound. It is made from positively charged sodium ions and negatively charged chloride ions. When solid salt dissolves in water, it splits into sodium and chloride ions.

Molecular compounds, such as sugar, are formed when atoms share their electrons. They also break up when they dissolve. However, they separate into uncharged molecules.

Electric Currents

Because they are charged, dissolved ions will carry an electric current through a solution. For this reason, ionic solutions are a type of electrolyte—a liquid that carries electricity. Molecular solutions do not contain any charged particles, so they do not conduct electric currents.

Measuring by Concentration

The amount of solute in a given quantity of solvent is measured as the concentration. Knowing the concentration is useful. Chemists can compare solutions or mix substances in a precise way.

Concentration is measured in many different ways. Chemists can express concentration in three ways: molarity, molality, and mole fraction.

Molarity (M) is the most common way chemists

KEY TERMS

Compound: A substance that contains two or more elements joined together by chemical bonds.
Electrolyte: An ionic substance that can conduct electricity.
Electron: A negatively charged particle that travels outside an atom's nucleus.
Immiscible: When substances cannot mix.
Ion: An atom that has lost or gained an electron or electrons.
Miscible: When substances can mix.
Molecule: A collection of two or more atoms that are connected by bonds.
Solution: A homogeneous mixture where substances are in the same physical state.
Solvent: A substance in which a solute is dissolved.

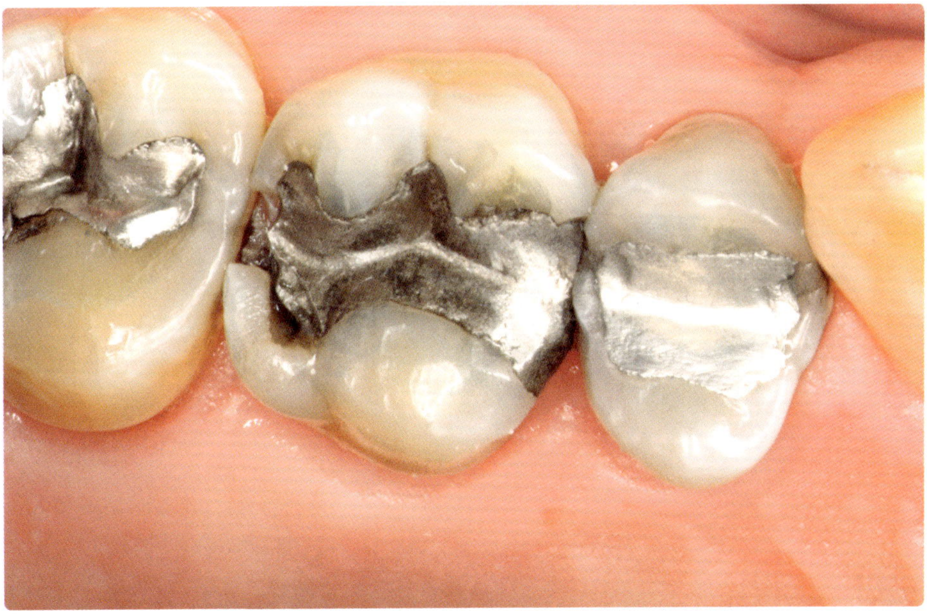

↑ These teeth have been repaired with metal fillings. The fillings are made from amalgam, an alloy in which silver and gold are dissolved in mercury.

DISSOLVING A SOLID

You can watch a solid dissolving in a liquid with this simple activity. You will need a tall, clear drinking glass; a powdered fruit drink; and a flat toothpick. Select a fruit drink with a dark color, such as grape or cherry.

1. Fill the glass with water.

2. Use the wide, flat end of the toothpick to pick up a small amount of fruit powder.

3. Gently shake the crystals of powder into the water in the glass.

4. Observe the crystals of the powder as they fall into the glass.

The tiny grains of powdered fruit drink are the solute. You can see them dissolve in the water because they create a colored solution. The color will spread out from the crystals and eventually fill the whole glass. This occurs due to a process called diffusion. Diffusion makes a liquid or gas spread out. This results from the random motion of the molecules making up the gas or liquid, as in Brownian motion.

express concentration. The molarity of solution is defined as the number of moles of solute in 1 liter (0.26 gallons) of solvent. One mole contains 602,213,670,000,000,000,000,000 (6.022×10^{23}) atoms or molecules. To calculate molarity, you find the number of moles of the solute and divide by the number of liters of solution. Molality is a similar measure of concentration.

← Tea is a solution that forms when chemicals in dried tea leaves dissolve in hot water. Strong tea has a higher concentration of these chemicals than weak tea.

Molality (m) is the number of moles of solute dissolved in a kilogram (2.2 pounds) of solvent. Molality is more accurate than molarity in some ways. As a liquid changes temperature, the volume will also change slightly. Molality is based on the mass of the solvent, not its volume, so it is the same no matter what the temperature is. Molarity is based on volume and will change slightly with temperature.

Mole fraction is a third way to measure concentration. It is the ratio of the number of moles of one substance in a solution to the total number of moles of all the substances in the solution. Adding all the

KEY TERMS

Concentration: The quantity of solute in a given amount of solvent.
Diffusion: The process that makes particles of gas or liquid spread out.
Molality: The number of moles of solute dissolved in one kilogram of solvent.
Molarity: The number of moles of solute dissolved in one liter of solvent.
Mole: 6.022×10^{23} particles of a substance.
Mole fraction: The ratio of the number of moles of one substance to the total moles of all the substances present.

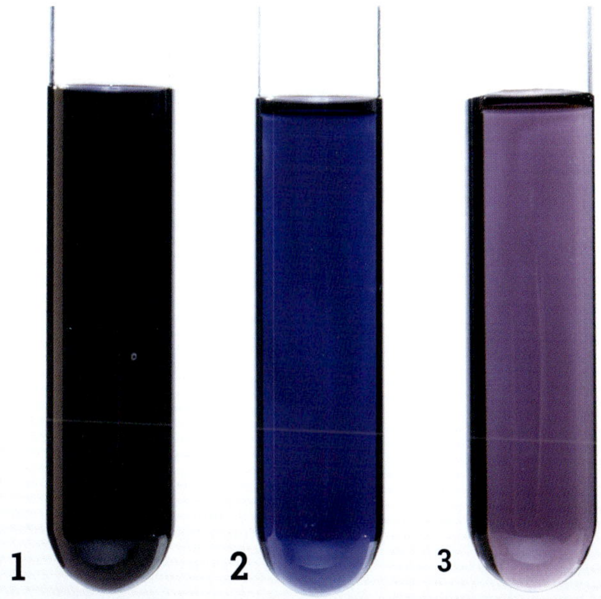

These three test tubes contain a starch solution. When a few drops of iodine are added to the starch, it changes color. The exact color depends on the concentration of the starch. High concentrations make the mixture turn a very dark blue-black (**1**). Low concentrations are purple (**3**), while medium-strength solutions produce a blue color (**2**).

fractions together always equals 1. The mole fraction is not affected by the temperature of the solution.

Saturation and Solubility

When a solute is added to a solution, only so much of it can dissolve in the solvent. When the maximum amount of solute has dissolved, the solution is said to be saturated. If you add a lot of sugar to a glass of warm water, some of the sugar will not dissolve in the water no matter how hard you stir. The water has become saturated with sugar, and

KEY TERMS

Saturated: A solution that has the maximum amount of solute dissolved in the solvent.
Solubility: A measure of how well a solute will dissolve in a solvent in specific conditions.

↓ Steam is hotter than boiling water, so more coffee dissolves into it to produce a concentrated solution.

SOLUBILITY

The effects of how the surface area of a substance affects its solubility can be seen by comparing how fast granulated sugar and a sugar cube dissolve in water.

1. Granulated sugar has a greater surface area in contact with the solvent, so it dissolves faster than a sugar cube.

2. Stirring increases the rate at which the solute dissolves because it sweeps heavy concentrations of dissolved sugar away from the undissolved sugar, so fresh unsaturated solvent can come into contact with it.

Solvent molecules have a greater kinetic energy at higher temperatures. When the solvent molecules are moving faster, they come in contact with more of the solute. This increases the rate of dissolving.

the remaining sugar stays in the bottom of the glass.

Solubility is defined as the amount of a solute that will dissolve in a solvent under a given set of conditions. A substance's solubility changes as the conditions change. For example, you can dissolve more sugar in hot water than in cold.

Determining Solubility

A substance's solubility is determined by the nature of the solute and the solvent. For example, solutes and solvents are either polar or nonpolar. Molecules that are polar have small electric charges at certain locations. These locations are known as poles—like the north and south poles of a magnet. Nonpolar molecules do not have poles. Polar molecules form when some atoms in the molecule attract electrons more strongly than other atoms. The electrons gather at one pole, making it negatively charged. The other end of the molecule becomes the positively charged pole.

The general rule is "like dissolves like." A solvent that has polar molecules will dissolve a solute with polar molecules. However, a polar solvent will not dissolve a solute that has nonpolar molecules.

Water is a polar solvent. It dissolves polar solutes, including ionic compounds. Salt dissolves easily in water. However, gasoline is a nonpolar solvent, so salt will not dissolve in it.

Temperature and pressure also affect solubility. Temperature has a stronger effect than pressure. In general, the higher the temperature, the more solute that will dissolve in a solvent. There are a number of factors that determine exactly how temperature affects solubility.

The speed at which a solid solute dissolves in a solvent is affected by three factors: how quickly the solute and solvent are mixed, the

MAKING ICE CREAM

Ice cream is a solution of frozen milk and flavorings. To make ice cream, you will need 2 cups of milk, ¼ cup of sugar, 2 teaspoons of vanilla extract, 4 cups of ice, ½ cup of salt, 2 Ziploc bags (one large and one small), and some duct tape.

1. Put the milk, sugar, and vanilla in a small Ziploc bag. Tape it shut and shake the bag to mix the ingredients.

2. Mix the ice cubes and salt in the large Ziploc bag.

3. Push the small Ziploc bag into the ice in the large Ziploc bag so it is surrounded with as much ice as possible.

4. Shake the large bag until the ingredients in the small bag change consistency.

5. Remove the small Ziploc bag and enjoy your ice cream!

Salt lowers the temperature of the ice in the bag. It is cold enough to freeze the milk and sugar to make ice cream.

temperature, and the total surface area of the solute. A fine powder will dissolve more quickly than a single large piece.

Physical Properties of a Solution

Sometimes the properties of a solution are different than those of the pure solvent. An obvious example is that the solvent may change color when a solute dissolves in it.

Adding a solute may also change the solvent's melting and boiling points. For example, pure water freezes at 32°Fahrenheit (0°C) and boils at 212°F (100°C). However, when salt is dissolved in water, the solution's melting point goes down and the boiling point goes up. The exact temperatures depend on how much salt is dissolved. For example, seawater freezes at about 0°F (–17.5°C). The reason why the melting point changes is because the solute gets in the way of the molecules of solvent.

In pure liquid water, the molecules are always moving and colliding with each other. When the water is at 32°F (0°C), the molecules begin to cling together when they collide. Soon they freeze into solid ice. However, as molecules join with the ice, others are breaking free and rejoining the liquid. At the freezing point, the same number of molecules freeze as melt. Below the freezing point, more of them freeze than melt, and the piece of ice grows in size.

When salt ions are mixed in, the water molecules cannot collide with each other as often. Some of the time they hit sodium or chloride ions. At 32°F (0°C), the water does not freeze because the molecules do not come together often enough. Those that do form into solid ice are outnumbered by the molecules turning into liquid, so ice does not build up.

What Are Suspensions?

Not all mixtures in nature are solutions. A suspension is a heterogeneous mixture in which large particles are spread throughout a liquid or a gas. The particles are large enough to settle out eventually. When you shake a snow globe, the pretend snow floating inside forms a suspension. It slowly settles back to the bottom.

The particles floating in a suspension can also stop light from passing through the suspension. This makes suspensions cloudy and difficult to see through. An example of this is muddy water, a suspension of grains of soil floating in water.

Suspensions can form from a mixture of solids, liquid, or gases.

An aerosol is a suspension

↑ Rock salt is used on roads during cold conditions. The salt melts the ice that forms on the surface of the road and prevents the water from refreezing. Ice is dangerous for drivers because it can cause them to skid.

EXPERIMENT WITH SUSPENSION

You can separate the liquid and solid in a suspension in this simple activity. You will need a large empty tin can, such as a coffee can, and some string. Ask an adult to help, and watch out: You might get wet!

1. Make two small holes in the can. The holes should be opposite each other near to the rim. Make sure the can's rim does not have a dangerous sharp edge. Push the string through the holes and tie them to make a long handle.

2. Fill the can about half full of water and add a handful of soil. Stir the water to mix in the soil and form a suspension. Take the can outside into an area with plenty of space.

3. Swing it around by the string at least 20 times. Be sure to hold on tightly to the string.

4. Without shaking the can, pour some of the water from the can into a glass and observe. If the water is still very cloudy, spin the can around again several more times.

The fine particles in the soil form a suspension in the water. When the can is swung, the spinning pushes the particles toward the bottom, speeding up the settling process. The can and string are a simple centrifuge. Centrifuges are spinning machines that remove suspended substances from liquids or gases.

A river winds through a forest. River water is a suspension of mud and silt. Faster-flowing rivers have larger particles suspended in them. As the river gets wider and slows down, the larger particles settle on the bottom.

Fog covers the slopes of a mountain. Fog is a colloid with tiny droplets of water spread out in the air. Fog and mist are the same thing; fog is just thicker.

of droplets of liquid or grains of solid in a gas. This type of mixture is created by spray cans. Solids are often suspended in liquids, but two liquids can also form a suspension. The liquids must be immiscible, such as oil and water. One of the liquids forms into tiny droplets, which are suspended in the other. This sort of suspension is called an emulsion.

What Are Colloids?

Colloids are mixtures that share the properties of both solutions and suspensions. The particles in a colloid are spread out through the solvent. They are larger than molecules or ions, but they are not heavy enough to settle. They are also too small to be filtered out. Colloids are common in nature. Milk, mayonnaise, and smoke are colloids.

CHAPTER 5

Solids and Their Properties

Solids are a state of matter with a fixed shape and volume. They are rigid and cannot be compressed easily. The particles are all linked together so they can vibrate, but they cannot flow.

Solids are around us everywhere: The ground is solid, buildings are solid, your shoes are solid, and much more. According to the kinetic theory—the theory that describes the movement of atoms and molecules—the particles of a solid are constantly moving. However, the particles within solids are held in place, and this is what gives them their fixed shape. Instead of moving around like the particles in a liquid or gas, the particles in a solid vibrate back and forth around a fixed central position.

↑ A closeup of sugar crystals. Each individual crystal has an ordered shape.

Solids have properties related to the arrangement of their particles. Because the particles of a solid are held firmly together, solids have a definite volume and shape. Unlike liquids or gases, in which the particles are able to move, the volume and shape of a solid does not change much with temperature or pressure. The arrangement of particles affects the properties of solids.

THREE UNIT CELLS FOUND IN CRYSTAL LATTICES

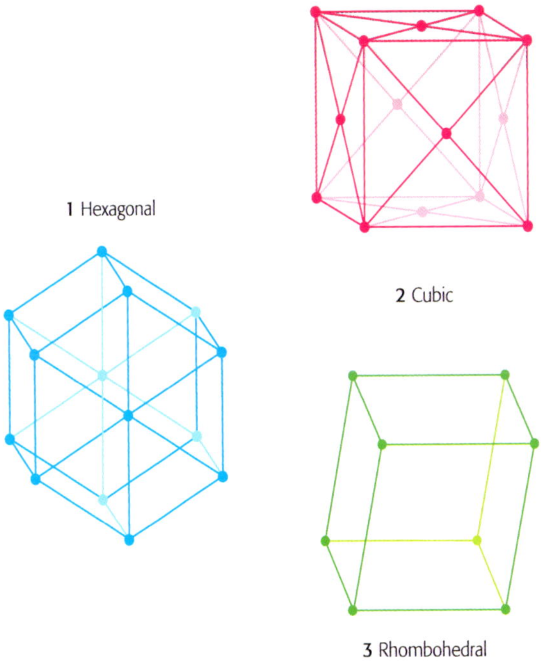

1. A hexagonal unit cell has 14 particles arranged in a shape with eight faces. Two of the faces are six-sided hexagons.

2. Cubic crystals have six square faces. The cube can contain eight, nine, or 14 particles (as shown here).

3. The rhombohedral cell has eight particles that make a six-faced shape. Each face is a rhombus.

Crystalline Solids

The most common types of solids are called crystalline solids. They are more often simply called crystals. Crystalline solids have highly ordered, repeating patterns of particles. These form a structure called a lattice. Table salt, sugar, bath salts, and snow are examples of everyday crystalline solids. Almost all precious gems are also crystalline solids.

Every crystal has a specific lattice structure. Many of a crystal's properties, such as how hard it is, are defined by how the lattice is put together. Chemists describe the lattice's pattern by selecting the smallest grouping of particles. This grouping is called the unit cell. The lattice is built of many unit cells linked together in a fixed pattern.

Chemists have found that there are just seven fundamental ways that a unit cell can be arranged. All crystals are built using one of these unit cells, which are cubic, hexagonal, rhombohedral, orthorhombic, tetragonal, monoclinic, or triclinic in shape.

Natural Solids

Crystals are very common in nature. Most nonliving solids are composed of crystals. Crystals are perhaps most familiar as the minerals in rocks. In nature, crystals grow from molten (melted) rock or solutions of saturated water. Some types of crystals can

EXAMINING SALT CRYSTALS

Crystals are made up of repeating patterns of atoms called unit cells. The unit cells are joined together in a larger, repeating pattern to form a structure called a lattice. The lattice can be broken down into smaller and smaller pieces, but each piece will still have the same repeating structure of unit cells.

1. Sprinkle some table salt crystals onto a dark surface. Observe the crystals with a magnifying glass. What shape are the crystals?

2. Sprinkle some pieces of rock salt onto a dark surface. Observe the crystals with a magnifying glass. How does the shape of the crystals compare to the table salt?

3. Tap one of the rock salt crystals with a hammer to break it up. Observe the crystals with the magnifying glass. How do they look now? You should see that all types of salt have the same cube-shaped crystals. When you shatter the large cubes of rock salt, you will see that it breaks into smaller cubes.

grow to a very large size. Single crystals have been found that are as big as a house and weigh many tons.

When crystals grow, they usually follow the same shape as their unit cell. For example, iron pyrite, a shiny gold-colored crystal also known as fool's gold, has a cube-shaped unit cell. Iron pyrite crystals are also cubes. Emerald crystals have a hexagon-shaped unit cell. A hexagon is a six-sided shape, and emeralds are often this shape, too.

When crystals break, they tend to break along the links between the unit cells. So, crystals break into certain shapes. Many minerals look very similar. One of the ways a geologist can identify a mineral is by looking at the way its crystal breaks apart.

PATTERNS

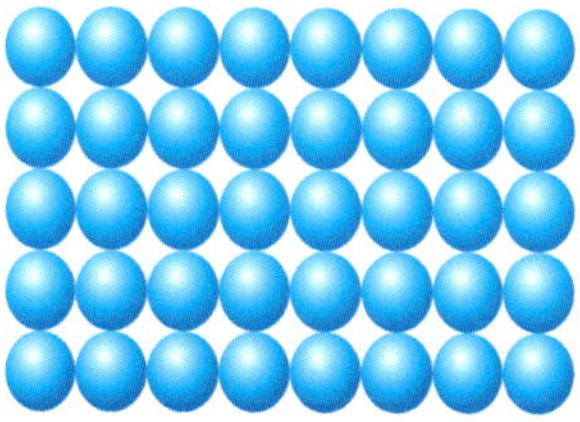

▲ A crystalline solid has molecules arranged in an ordered pattern.

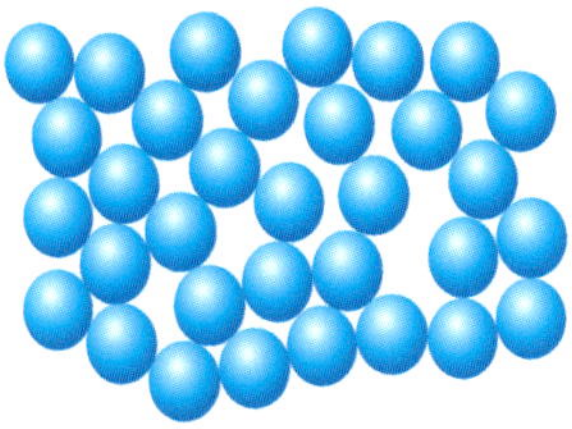

▲ In an amorphous solid, the molecules are all linked together but are arranged in a random pattern.

Amorphous Solids

The word amorphous means "without shape." It is used to describe objects that do not have a definite shape but can take many shapes. Some solids are described as amorphous. They do not have particles arranged in an ordered lattice. Common examples of amorphous solids are plastics and rubber.

Without a lattice structure, amorphous solids have different properties than crystals. For example, most crystals are hard and shatter easily when they are hit. The bits of broken crystal are also the same shape. Amorphous solids tend to be more flexible. If they are broken, the pieces are all different shapes and sizes.

Some amorphous solids, such as glass, are actually supercooled liquids. Rather than being thought of as solids, they can be thought of as extremely viscous liquids. These liquids are so viscous that they do not flow and can hold their shape like a solid. However, like a liquid, the materials can take any shape.

KEY TERMS

Amorphous: Something that lacks a definite structure or shape.

Crystal: A solid made of regular repeating patterns of atoms.

Solution: A mixture of substances where all ingredients are mixed evenly.

Supercooled liquid: An extremely viscous liquid that flows so slowly, it can hold its shape like a solid.

Viscous: A viscous liquid is one that is not very runny and flows slowly.

These used plastic bottles are undergoing the recycling process. Plastic is an amorphous solid and can be molded into almost any shape.

This link to liquids is also shown when amorphous solids are heated. Crystalline solids have a fixed melting point. At this temperature, the whole crystal turns quickly into a liquid. When amorphous solids are heated, they become soft and might flow into a different shape before finally melting into a runny liquid.

Properties of Solids

The physical properties of gases and liquids are explained by the strength of the forces between particles. These forces also explain the physical properties of solids. These include hardness, ability to conduct electricity, and melting point. Each of these properties depends on the strength of the forces holding the solid together.

↑ Some instruments, such as trumpets, are made from brass. Brass is an alloy of copper and zinc. The alloy can be molded, rolled, and hammered into a range of shapes. It does not corrode or discolor quickly.

KEY TERMS

Alloy: A solid solution of two or more metals.
Ductile: When a solid can be drawn into wire.
Malleable: When a material can be beaten into a flat sheet.
Valence electrons: The electrons in the outer shell of an atom.

GOLDEN CHEMISTRY

The purity of gold and other precious metals is measured in karats. Pure gold has 24 karats. Jewelry is seldom made of pure gold because it is very soft and can be dented or bent easily. Most jewelry is made from a gold alloy, which contains copper and other metals to make it harder. You often see jewelry identified as 18 karat, 14 karat, or 12 karat. The number of karats shows the percentage of gold in the alloy. Twenty-four-karat gold is 100 percent gold. Jewelry made from 18-karat gold contains 75 percent gold, while 12-karat gold is just 50 percent gold. The percentage is arrived at using the following equation:

$$(\text{Number of karats} \div 24) \times 100 = \text{percentage of pure gold}$$

So, for 18-karat gold the equation looks like this:

$(18 \div 24) \times 100 = 75$ percent

For 12-karat gold the value is:

$(12 \div 24) \times 100 = 50$ percent

This is the mask of Tutankhamen, an Egyptian king who was buried more than 3,000 years ago. The mask is made from pure (24-karat) gold.

Metals

Metals are common solids. Approximately three-quarters of all elements are metals. Metals usually have a small number of valence electrons available for bonding. Valence electrons are those in the outer shell of an atom. These are the electrons involved in chemical bonds. When metal atoms form into a lattice, the valence electrons break free of the atoms and move freely inside the solid. The free electrons act as a "glue" that holds the metal atoms together. The electrons can be made to flow in one direction, forming an electric current. Metals are excellent conductors. As well as carrying electricity, metals also conduct heat well.

Metals have two other properties: malleability and ductility. A malleable material can be shaped or extended into thin sheets by beating. Ductile materials can be drawn into wire. Both of these properties result from the way the free electrons "glue" the metal atoms together.

Alloys

Metals are very useful. They are strong and can be molded into any shape. Metals are used for a wide variety of objects, including cars, wires, buildings, rockets, and jewelry, and many other products.

Sometimes a pure metal does not have the properties needed for a given task. It may be too soft or not flexible enough. One way to make a metal more useful is to mix it with other metals. A mixture of metals is called an alloy. Brass is an alloy of copper and zinc. Some alloys contain nonmetals. Steel is an alloy of iron and several other metals, and it also contains small amounts of carbon.

Alloys are a solution of metals with one metal dissolved in another. For example, solder is an alloy with tin atoms dissolved in lead. Solder is a soft alloy that melts easily. It is used to fuse pieces of metal together.

The Golden Gate Bridge in California is made from steel. Steel is a very tough alloy of iron and carbon.

KEY TERMS

Compound: A substance formed in a chemical reaction when the atoms of two or more elements bond into a molecule.
Ion: An atom that has lost or gained electrons. Ions have either a positive or negative charge.
Molecule: A group of two or more bonded atoms that forms the smallest unit of a substance.

Molecular Solids

Many solids are made of molecules. Molecules are groups of two or more atoms bonded together. A few elements form

The electric cables shown here are made from aluminum. This metal is a good conductor and is very light. The cables are held in place on the pylon by insulators made from nonmetal molecular solids called ceramics. Insulators do not conduct electricity.

molecular solids, including sulfur and iodine. Most molecular solids are compounds. Compounds form when two or more elements react with each other. Their atoms bond together to make a molecule. Sugar is an example of a compound that forms a molecular solid.

Molecular solids are held together by the forces between molecules. In general, molecular solids are soft and melt at low temperatures. This is because the forces between the molecules tend to be weak. Most do not conduct electricity or heat well.

Ionic Solids

Some compounds are formed from ions. Ions are atoms that have lost or gained

IONIC SOLID

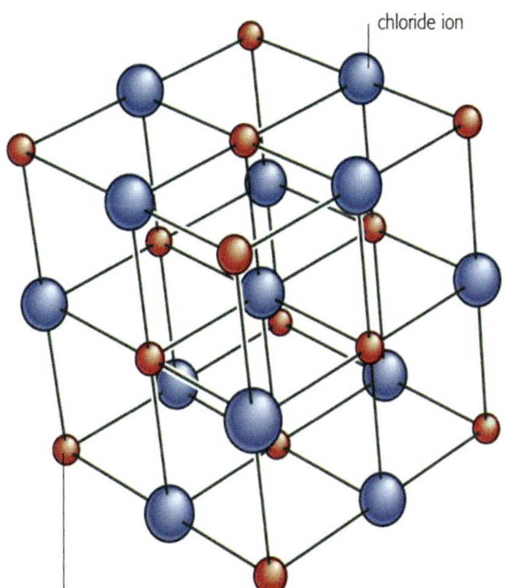

Sodium chloride lattice

electrons during a chemical reaction. All ions have a charge. Ions that have lost electrons have a positive charge. Ions that have gained electrons have a negative charge.

Opposite charges attract each other, and like charges repel (push away from) each other. An ion in a solid is attracted to another ion with the opposite charge. This attraction is what holds ionic solids together. However, the ions are also repelling those with the same charge.

Ionic solids are crystalline. The ions are arranged in a lattice. Inside the lattice, the ions are arranged so ions with opposite charges are as close together as possible. Ions with the same charge are as far apart as possible.

Ionic solids are hard because of their crystalline lattice. Also, because the ionic bonds are so strong, the solids have high melting points, usually much higher than molecular solids. Ionic solids are poor conductors because the ions cannot move.

The simplest ionic solids are made of two ions: one positive and the other negative. A common example is table salt, or sodium chloride. Sodium chloride has one positively charged sodium ion for every negatively charged chloride ion.

THE CHARGE OF IONS

When writing the formula for an ionic compound, you need to know the charge of the ions involved. Metal ions always have a positive charge, and nonmetals always produce negatively charged ions. The name of the ion can provide a clue about the charge. Positive ions have the same name as the atoms (for example, sodium ion), but negative ions often have a different name (for example, chloride ion).

Ion	Symbol	Charge
sodium	Na^{+}	+1
potassium	K^{+}	+1
calcium	Ca^{2+}	+2
aluminum	Al^{3+}	+3
chloride	Cl^{-}	−1
oxide	O^{2-}	−2
phosphate	PO_4^{3-}	−3

When writing the formula, the charge of the compound must be equal to zero. For example, potassium chloride is made up of potassium ions and chloride ions. A potassium ion has a charge of +1 and a chloride ion has a charge of −1. Therefore, one of each ion combines to form the molecule, which has the formula KCl.

Aluminium chloride is made up of aluminium and chloride ions. Because the aluminium ion has a charge of +3 and the chloride ion has a charge of −1, an aluminium ion combines with three chloride ions. The chemical formula for aluminium chloride is $AlCl_3$. The number 3 shows that the molecule has three chloride ions for one aluminium ion. Together the chloride ions have a total charge of −3, which balances the +3 charge of the aluminium ion.

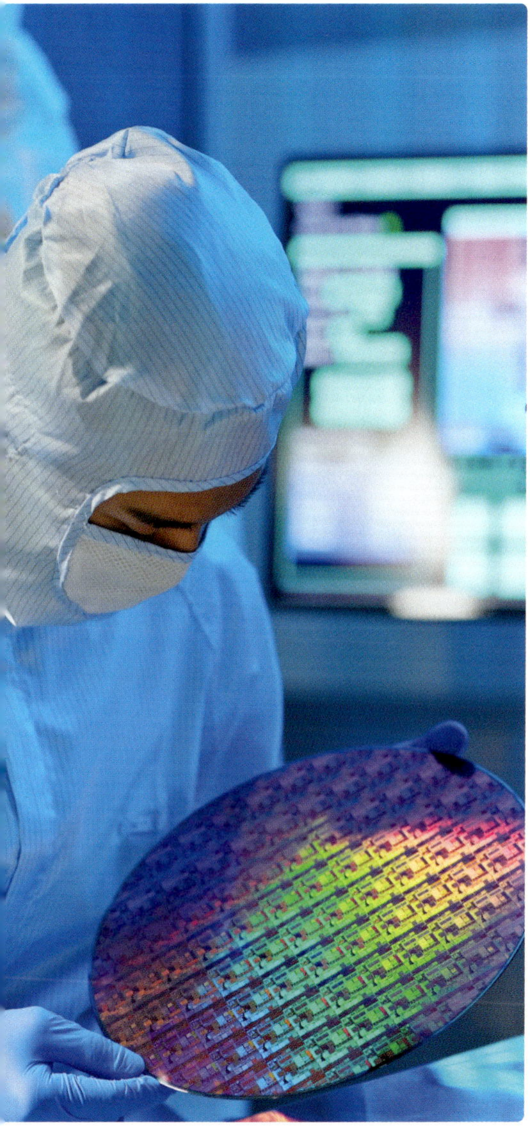

↑ A technician inspects a wafer of silicon. The wafer has been etched with tiny electric circuits to be used as microchips. Microchips are made from silicon and other solid metalloids. They are used in computers, washing machines, televisions, and almost every other type of electronic device.

FORMULA FUN

Use the information in the box on page 56 to make the chemical formulas for these ionic compounds:

calcium oxide

sodium phosphate

calcium phosphate

Strong Solids

Some solids have atoms strongly bonded to each other with covalent bonds. Covalent bonds are formed when atoms share their valence electrons. Many covalent solids are molecular. However, some are crystalline. The covalent bonds connect all the atoms to form a lattice. The lattice is a very strong structure that is difficult to break. This type of solid is called a covalent-network solid. The physical properties of covalent-network solids include a high melting point. Diamonds are an example of covalent-network solids.

Metalloids

The metalloids are a small group of elements that have some of the properties of metals and some of the properties of nonmetals. Metalloids include silicon and arsenic. One property of metalloids is that they conduct electricity, but only in certain conditions. Therefore, these materials are called semiconductors. Semiconductors have become important since the 1960s. They are used in electronic devices, such as transistors and diodes, which control the flow of electricity around a circuit. Electronics make it possible to build small computers, cell phones, and similar machines.

Semiconductors form covalent-network solids. The atoms are arranged into a lattice. Inside a pure semiconductor, there are just the right number of electrons to form covalent bonds between all the atoms. However, the electrons are held only loosely in these bonds. A few escape from the bonds and can flow through the solid to conduct electricity. The empty places, known as holes, left by the missing electrons can also move about. The holes behave like movable positive charges.

The way semiconductors conduct electricity can be controlled by adding atoms of other elements. This is a process known as doping. The doping process fills in the gaps in the lattice of metalloid atoms with an atom of a different element.

Mercury is the only metal to be a liquid at room temperature. It expands more than any other metal when it is heated. This property used to be used in thermometers. As the mercury heated up, it expanded and moved up inside the thermometer, showing the rise in temperature. Most countries have banned mercury for use in home thermometers because mercury is toxic to people and animals. If the thermometer breaks, it can cause serious health problems.

ALLOTROPES

Pure carbon exists in more than one form, or allotrope. The two common carbon allotropes are diamond and graphite, which is used as pencil lead. Both allotropes are pure carbon, but the atoms are arranged differently. This gives the solids very different properties.

Diamonds are the hardest substance known, while graphite is very soft. In both forms, each carbon atom is bonded to four others. In diamond, each atom is bonded strongly to its four neighbors. The atoms form a three-dimensional network, which is very rigid. This structure is what makes diamonds so hard. In graphite, each atom is strongly bonded to just three of its neighbors. Together, the atoms form layers of hexagons. The atom's fourth bond is with an atom included in another layer. This bond is much weaker, and that allows the layers to move over one another. Graphite is soft because its layers of atoms can move around easily. For example, the mark left by a pencil is a layer of graphite being rubbed onto the paper.

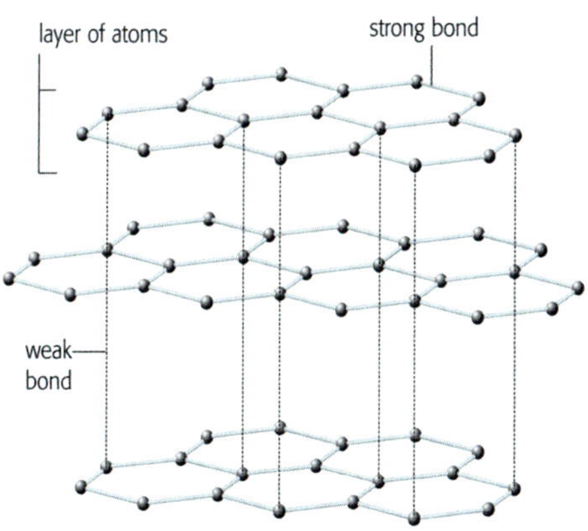

In graphite, the carbon atoms form hexagons that connect into sheets. The sheets are only weakly linked together, so they can move past each other easily.

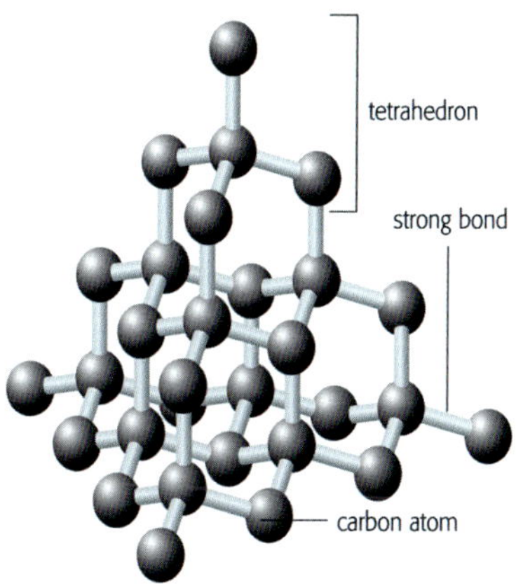

In diamond, ach carbon atom is joined to four others. Together a unit of five atoms forms a very strong pyramid structure called a tetrahedron.

For example, pure silicon can conduct only a small amount of electricity. If silicon is doped with phosphorus, four of the five electrons of the phosphorus atom bond with silicon atoms. The fifth electron is left free. This free electron is able to move through the solid and carry a current.

Expanding Solids

The change from a liquid to a solid is called freezing, and the change from a solid to a liquid is called melting. Before they melt, solids expand as they are heated. As the solid gets hotter, the atoms inside vibrate more, and the distance between the atoms increases.

As a result, the entire solid expands. Crystalline and molecular solids tend to expand only a small amount. In general, it is metals that expand the most. Large metal structures, such as bridges, must be designed so their metal sections can expand during hot days.

A cloud of carbon dioxide gas subliming from a piece of dry ice (solid carbon dioxide). Carbon dioxide is actually colorless, but in this case the gas is so cold that it makes the water vapor in the air form a mist of tiny droplets. Carbon dioxide is also a heavy gas, so it sinks to the floor.

Solid to Gas

A few solids do not melt. Instead, they change from a solid directly into a gas. This process is called sublimation.

Evaporation is when a liquid turns to a gas. In this process, all the atoms or molecules separate from each other and move around independently. Under some circumstances, the molecules in a solid have enough energy to become a gas in the same way.

Molecular solids are the most likely to sublime. These solids are held together by weak forces between the molecules, so it is easier for individual molecules to break free and form a gas. Iodine forms a shiny gray molecular solid. When it is heated, the element sublimes into a deep-purple gas. Another common solid that sublimes is dry ice. Dry ice is the name for frozen carbon dioxide. It is a white solid and looks a lot like water ice. However, as its name suggests, it does not make things wet. Dry ice is used to keep food and other delicate items cold but also dry.

Water ice can sometimes sublime. If you leave an ice cube in the freezer for a long time, it can sublime. The air inside the freezer has very little water vapor in it. This makes it easier for molecules of water to break off from the solid ice and form vapor. (If the air was already filled with water vapor, the ice would not sublime as easily.)

Another example of sublimation is solid air freshener used to make a room smell nice. The air freshener sublimes and releases a gas that covers up odors.

KEY TERMS

Allotrope: One of several solid forms of an element. Allotropes all contain the same type of atom, but they are arranged differently.
Hole: The space left by an electron that has been freed from a semiconductor's lattice.
Semiconductor: A material that conducts electricity under certain conditions.
Sublimation: The process by which a solid turns into a gas without becoming a liquid.

CHAPTER 6

Changing the Basic States of Matter

The basic states of matter are solids, liquids, and gases. Matter can be made to change state. A change of state is a physical change, involves a change in heat, and is reversible. Changes are made by adding or removing energy.

A change in state, or phase change, happens when a substance turns from one phase to another—for example, when a solid becomes a liquid. A phase change happens when particles in solids, liquids, or gases either combine or break up. These phase changes always involve a change in energy.

Phase Changes

When a substance undergoes a phase change from solid to liquid or liquid to gas, the particles must overcome the intermolecular forces—the forces between molecules—in the original state. The energy particles used to overcome the intermolecular forces is kinetic

→ This spiderweb is hung with beads of dew. Dew forms when moist air cools or hits a cold surface and condenses (turns into a liquid). This switch from air to water represents a change of state, or phase change.

KEY TERMS

Endothermic: A chemical reaction in which heat is absorbed and the surrounding temperature falls.
Exothermic: A chemical reaction in which heat is released and the surrounding temperature goes up.
Heat of fusion: The amount of energy needed to turn a solid into a liquid.
Heat of vaporization: The amount of energy needed to turn a liquid into a gas.
Phase change: A change from one state to another.

energy. The source of this kinetic energy is heat. As heat is added to a substance, the particles absorb the energy and increase their own kinetic energy. Temperature is a measure of the average kinetic energy. Therefore, there is a temperature increase when more energy is added.

When a substance undergoes a phase change from gas to liquid or liquid to solid, energy is also important. However, the particles must lose kinetic energy. The particles move more slowly as the phase changes. Because energy is given up, this is called an endothermic process.

Changing a substance from a liquid to a gas requires more energy than changing the same substance from a solid to a liquid. Gases have the highest energy of the three states of matter. The substance must gain enough kinetic energy for the particle to completely overcome the intermolecular forces. Substances that have stronger

When ice cream melts, it is undergoing a change of state from solid to liquid. Heat from the atmosphere breaks the intermolecular bonds that hold the molecules firmly together as a frozen solid.

intermolecular forces have higher boiling points because more energy is required for the particles to become a gas.

The amount of energy that is needed to change a solid to a liquid is called the heat of fusion. The amount of energy required to change a liquid to a gas is called the heat of vaporization.

WATER EXPANSION

Materials: small bowl, clear drinking straw, food coloring, eyedropper, modeling clay, permanent marker

1. Press a piece of clay onto the bottom of the bowl.

2. Push the drinking straw into the clay so that the straw stands up.

3. Add several drops of food coloring to some water. Use the eyedropper to fill the drinking straw until it is about half full of colored water.

4. Mark the level of the water in the straw with the permanent marker.

5. Place the bowl in the freezer for at least 4 hours.

6. Remove the bowl from the freezer and observe how the level in the straw has changed as the water froze. As the water froze, the ice expanded. This should have caused the level of the water in the straw to increase.

Mark the level of the water with a permanent marker.

The water in the straw has risen because water expands when it becomes ice. Almost every other substance contracts when it freezes.

This ceramic plant pot has cracked over the winter through the effects of freezing. As water in the soil froze, it expanded, and the increase in volume caused the pot to crack.

Solid to Liquid

The heat of fusion is the amount of energy needed to break the intermolecular bonds in a solid to turn it into a liquid. The change in phase from a solid to a liquid does not involve a change in temperature. While a substance is melting, the temperature remains constant. This means that while a substance is melting, the particles do not actually change their kinetic energy. There is not a change in the kinetic energy until the phase change is complete.

Frost forms on a window when there is moist air inside and temperatures below freezing point outside. The moist air changes state to form ice crystals.

Pressure cookers are used to cook food more quickly than simply boiling it. The increase in pressure raises the temperature of the liquid in the pot so the food takes less time to cook.

Liquid to Solid

The heat of fusion is also the amount of heat given off when a substance changes from a liquid to a solid. For most substances, the particles in the solid state are much closer together than in the liquid state. This means there are more molecules packed into a given volume in a solid than a liquid. The solid form of a substance therefore has a higher density than the liquid form. That explains why the solid phase for most substances will sink in its liquid phase.

Water is one of the exceptions to this rule. When water freezes, the water molecules actually move farther apart than they are in the liquid phase.

CHILL OUT

Evaporative cooling is an efficient way to lower temperature.

Materials: rubbing alcohol, cotton ball, safety thermometer

1. Pour a little rubbing alcohol onto the cotton ball.

2. Squeeze out the excess alcohol and lightly wrap the cotton ball around the bulb of the thermometer.

3. Blow on the cotton ball and watch what happens to the temperature on the thermometer. The alcohol absorbs energy so it can evaporate. This causes the temperature to decrease.

This occurs because of the strong intermolecular forces in water caused by hydrogen bonding. This explains why ice floats in water. Ice is actually about 9 percent less dense than water. Because water expands as it freezes, it is important to leave space in a container of water before freezing. If a full container is sealed, the water will expand and cause the container to burst.

When a solid is heated and it reaches the melting point, the temperature remains constant as the phase changes. Scientists can easily measure this temperature for substances that do not have very high or very low melting points. The melting point is the same temperature as the freezing point. When a liquid is cooled and it reaches the freezing point, the temperature remains constant until the phase changes. The melting point or freezing point of a substance may also be useful in determining the exact nature of a substance. Each substance has its own melting point.

KEY TERMS

Intermolecular force: The weak attraction between the molecules of a substance.

Melting point: The temperature at which a solid changes into a liquid. This same temperature is also called the freezing point when a liquid changes into a solid.

BOILING AND EVAPORATION

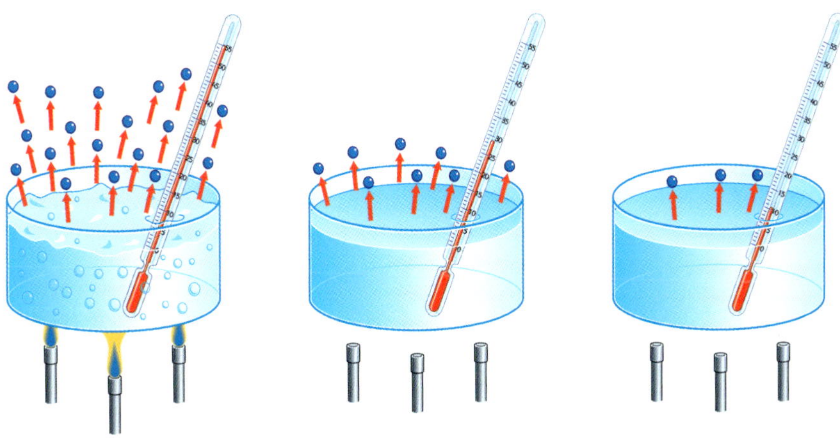

(a) Boiling: molecules driven off

(b) Evaporation: molecules escape

(c) Evaporation: causes cooling

When a liquid is boiled (a), the molecules gain kinetic energy and can escape from the surface and form vapor bubbles in the liquid. In evaporation (b), molecules leave the liquid without heat being added. The liquid loses energy and gets cooler (c).

KEY TERMS

Condensation: The change of state from a gas to a liquid.
Evaporation: The change of state from a liquid to a gas when the liquid is at a temperature below its boiling point.
Pressure: The force pushing on an area.
Vapor: The gas form of a substance that exists below the substance's critical temperature and can still be liquefied.

Liquid to Gas

As with melting, the temperature of this phase change remains constant until the phase change is complete. When a liquid reaches its boiling point, the particles do not gain kinetic energy. Instead, the particles in the liquid use the energy to overcome the intermolecular forces. Once all the liquid has changed to a gas, the temperature rises again.

Boiling Liquid

A liquid boils when its vapor pressure is equal to the atmospheric pressure. For example, at sea level, water boils at 212°F (100°C). As elevation above sea level increases, the atmospheric pressure decreases. This decrease in atmospheric pressure means that the temperature at which water boils also decreases. This decrease can become significant when cooking at higher elevations. Many recipes include directions for cooking the food at higher elevations.

If the atmospheric pressure is increased, the boiling point of water also increases. Some cooks use a device called a pressure cooker to increase the pressure and thereby increase the temperature at which water boils. Because the temperature is increased, the food cooks much faster.

Evaporative Cooling

The changing of a liquid to a gas requires energy. That is an endothermic process. This process is very important for survival. When you work hard or exercise, your body generates heat. Your body must rid itself of this excess heat. One way your body does this is by sweating. When your body heats up, sweat covers your skin. Heat from your body warms the sweat, causing it to begin evaporating. Because evaporation is an endothermic process, the sweat molecules absorb heat, and this creates a cooling effect on the body.

Cooling by evaporation (evaporative cooling) is a good way for your body to get rid of excess heat. However, cooling by evaporation does not always work. One factor that affects evaporative cooling is humidity. Humidity is the amount of water vapor present in the air. When the humidity is high, the amount of water vapor present in the air can approach the saturation point (maximum possible). In these conditions, air cannot hold any more water, and sweat cannot evaporate from the body. The most ideal condition for evaporative cooling is when the air has very little water vapor in it.

States of Water

Like all matter, water exists in three main states—solid, liquid, and gas. Water is familiar to us in all its different states.

When hot water vapor meets a cold surface, such as a window, it condenses (changes from a gas to a liquid) into drops of water.

Water as a solid is called ice, as a liquid it is just called water, and as a gas it is called water vapor or steam. As water changes between states, each of these changes has a name. When water changes from a solid to a liquid, it melts. When water changes from a liquid to a solid, it freezes. When water changes from a liquid to a gas, it boils. When water changes from a gas to a liquid, it condenses. Suppose you took an ice cube from the freezer. If the freezer is at 23°F (–5°C), the ice cube will be at the same temperature. If the ice cube is placed in a pan and heated on the stove, energy is added. The ice cube absorbs energy and its temperature increases steadily. When the ice cube reaches its melting point, the temperature does not change. Energy is being used to change the solid to a liquid so the temperature remains constant until all the ice melts.

Once the ice melts, the temperature rises again. The temperature of the water continues to rise until it reaches the boiling point. Once the water starts boiling, the temperature remains constant until all the water has changed to water vapor or steam. After all the water has boiled and turned to steam, the temperature of the steam increases as more energy is added.

When energy is removed from steam, the reverse happens. The temperature of the steam decreases until it begins to condense (change from gas to liquid). The temperature is constant until all the steam condenses into liquid water. The temperature continues to decrease until the water reaches its freezing point. As the water changes from a liquid to a solid, the temperature remains constant. Once all the water has turned to ice, the temperature continues to fall.

STATES OF WATER

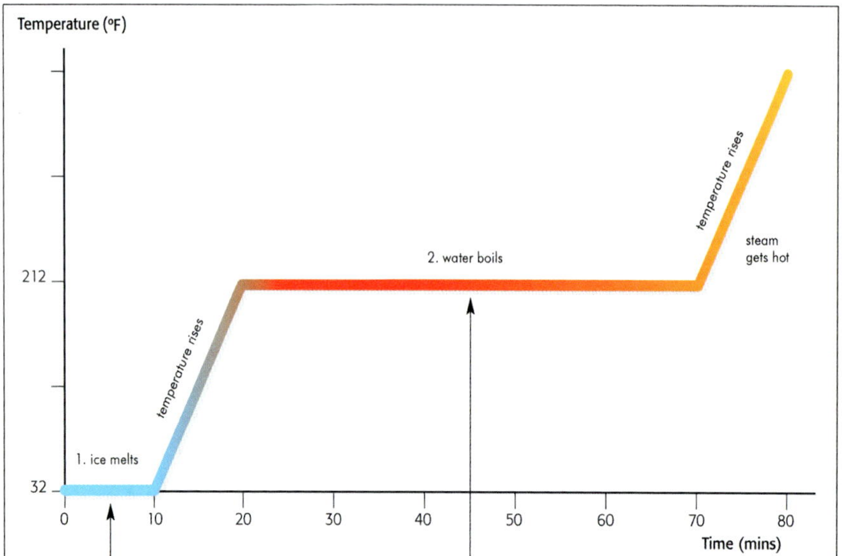

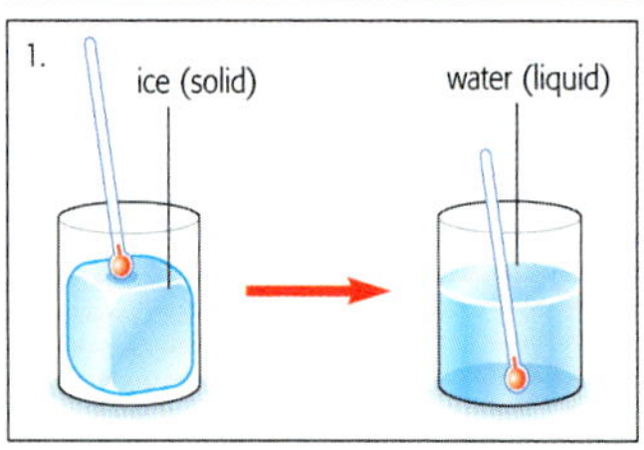

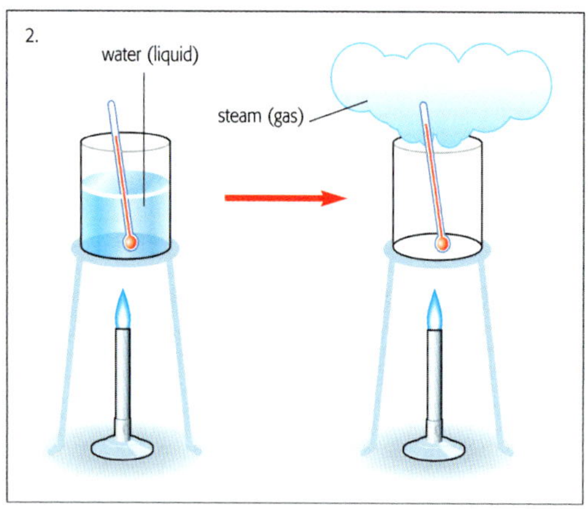

1. Changing state requires an input or release of energy. To melt ice, heat must be added. It takes 80 kilocalories of heat to melt 2.2 lbs (1 kg) of ice. While this is happening, the temperature remains at 32°F (0°C). Once all the ice has become liquid, the temperature begins to go up.

2. The change of state from liquid to gas requires further input of energy. Heat is needed to raise the temperature of the water to its boiling point of 212°F (100°C). It takes 54 minutes at a rate of 10 kilocalories per minute to turn 2.2 lbs (1 kg) of water into 2.2 lbs (1 kg) of steam. This quantity of energy is called the heat of vaporization, which for water equals 540 kcal/kg. During this time, the water remains at 212°F (100°C).

CHAPTER 7

BIOGRAPHY

Antoine Lavoisier

The French scientist Antoine Lavoisier revolutionized chemistry. Although he trained as a lawyer, his real love was science. He named the elements carbon, hydrogen, and oxygen, as well as discovering the role of oxygen in combustion and respiration. In 1794, he was branded a traitor by French revolutionaries and was sent to the guillotine.

"It required only a moment to sever his head and probably one hundred years will not suffice to produce another like it."

–Joseph-Louis Lagrange, mathematician

Antoine Laurent Lavoisier was born in Paris on August 26, 1743. As the son of a leading lawyer, Antoine was educated in law at the best school in Paris, the Collège Mazarin. Chemistry, mathematics, astronomy, and botany were also taught at the school. It was these subjects, rather than his legal studies, that fired the young scholar's imagination, and he soon began to devote his spare time to scientific experiments.

Education

Lavoisier graduated in 1763 but did not join the legal profession. Instead, he accepted an invitation to help the scientist Jean-Etienne Guettard (1715–1786) carry out a geological survey of France. The task took three years, at the end of which Lavoisier wrote a paper on the properties of gypsum, a mineral also known as "plaster of Paris" because it was used to cover the walls of Parisian houses. In 1765, he presented the paper at the foremost institution of learning

In this image, Lavoisier is pictured in his laboratory. In 1768, the Academy of Sciences in Paris tried to find out whether water supplied to Parisian citizens through an open canal was fit to drink. This started Lavoisier on a series of experiments he carried out on water.

in the country, the Academy of Sciences.

In 1766, Lavoisier entered an Academy competition to find a better system of street lighting for Paris. At this time, the only form of lighting in towns was with oil lamps or candles. The development of coal gas or electric lighting lay many decades in the future. Lavoisier's essay on various forms of lighting apparatus did not win him the prize, but its treatment of the subject so impressed the judges that King Louis XV (1710–1774) ordered him to be given a special medal. Lavoisier's name was already becoming known.

Fateful Decision

Lavoisier had received a large inheritance from his wealthy family, but he still needed a steady income to fund his scientific studies. To help with this, in 1768 (the same year he was elected to the Academy), he bought a stake in the General Farm (Ferme Générale), a tax-collecting agency used by the royal government to collect taxes on tobacco, salt, and other goods. Agency members, known as tax farmers, made great profits for themselves and were universally disliked. Their activities were a chief cause of grievance against the French monarchy in the years leading up to the French Revolution (1789–1799). Joining the Ferme Générale would prove to be a disastrous decision for Lavoisier.

Meanwhile, in 1771, at the age of 28, he married Marie-Anne Pierrette Paulze, the 14-year-old daughter of a fellow member of the agency. Despite the great age difference, the two shared an interest in science.

KEY DATES

1743	Born in Paris, France
1765	Publishes paper on gypsum
1768	Joins a private tax-collecting agency used by government
1770	Proves that water cannot be turned into earth
1772–75	Shows that metals burn by absorbing "vital principle" from air
1777	Identifies "dephlogisticated air" as oxygen
1783	Shows that water is a compound of hydrogen and oxygen
1785	Becomes director of the Academy of Sciences
1787	Defines concept of the chemical element and publishes *Method of Chemical Nomenclature*
1789	Publishes *Elementary Treatise of Chemistry*
1794	Condemned by revolutionary tribunal and guillotined

Marie-Anne helped Lavoisier in his laboratory experiments. Lavoisier's private fortune enabled him to purchase the best scientific equipment that money could buy. He prepared reports for the Academy of Sciences on diverse subjects, including early balloon flight, hypnotism, the manufacture of gunpowder, inks and dyes, and the reasons why iron rusts.

This 17th-century painting by David Teniers (1610–1690) shows an alchemist in his workshop. Alchemists had many goals, including trying to turn base metals into gold and silver.

Experiments with Water

In 1768, the Academy of Sciences decided to find out whether water supplied to Paris through an open canal was fit to drink. The usual way of testing for impurities was to boil water dry in order to see what solids were left. These investigations started Lavoisier on a new line of scientific inquiry: whether it was possible for one substance (water) to be changed into another (earth). According to the medieval alchemists—scholars who blended philosophy and mysticism with practical chemical experimentation—it was.

The idea that some substances could be changed (or "transmuted") into others when heated derived from Aristotle's theory of the four elements of water, earth, air, and fire. It lay at the root of the alchemists' age-old search for the "philosopher's stone" that would turn metals such as lead, tin, or copper into gold or silver. However, alchemy was not just a question of magic and mysticism. In many respects, it was the forerunner of chemistry; no less a scientist than Isaac Newton is known to have carried out alchemical experiments. Even in the late 18th century, some scientists were still prepared to argue that water turned into earth on heating. This was based on the fact that when pure rainwater was distilled (condensed) in a glass vessel, solid matter ("earth") was left behind. However, Lavoisier suspected that this "earth" was dissolved, or leached from, the glass itself during the boiling process.

Using some of the most sophisticated measuring devices available, Lavoisier weighed both the glass vessel and the water before and after heating, time after time, over a period of three months. He found that the weight of the residue of "earth" more or less equalled that lost by the vessel. As he had suspected, the "earth" had not come from the water, but had been produced from the glass apparatus itself.

The Phlogiston Theory

Lavoisier's attention then turned toward an investigation of what takes place when substances are burned (combustion). According to German chemist Georg Stahl, all substances were ultimately made up of water and three varieties of earth, one of which was combustible. This, he argued, was set free into the air when the substance was burned. He therefore called it phlogiston, from the Greek word for "burned." According to Stahl, metals burned because they lost phlogiston into the atmosphere, whereas we now know that the reverse is true: they burn by uniting with oxygen in the atmosphere.

> *"Chemists have made phlogiston a vague principle... sometimes it has weight, sometimes it has not, sometimes it is free fire, sometimes it is fire combined with an earth.... It is a veritable Proteus that changes its form for every instant!"*
>
> **—Lavoisier in an essay attacking the theory of phlogiston (1785)**

Lavoisier's interest in combustion first developed in 1771 when the amateur chemist Louis-Bernard Guyton de Morveau (1737–1816) showed that metals grew heavier when they were roasted in air. Guyton, in common with all scientists at that time, believed in Stahl's phlogiston theory. If phlogiston was lost during combustion, metals would lose weight. In order to make the facts fit with the theory, Guyton claimed that metals became heavier when "dephlogisticated" because phlogiston was a weightless substance that buoyed up the materials containing it. Lavoisier seriously doubted this conclusion. He thought that a more likely explanation was that "air" (the term then used for a gas) was somehow involved in the process of combustion, and that this air caused the increase in weight.

Combustion of Substances

Lavoisier burned a variety of substances in order to measure the changes in weight that took place. He reported his findings in November 1772 and concluded that phosphorus and sulfur increased in weight when burned because they absorbed air. He then reversed the process by roasting a burned metallic residue with charcoal. Scientists at the time called the crumbly residue left after a metal has been burned or roasted (calcinated) the calx. We now know it as an oxide (a compound formed when any substance mixes with oxygen). The metal after roasting weighed less than the original calx, suggesting to Lavoisier that it had lost the air absorbed in the original burning. Lavoisier used litharge, which is an oxide of lead, for these experiments.

Lavoisier now became aware that a group of chemists then at work in Britain had already discovered that the atmosphere is made up of several different "airs." These chemists are known as the "pneumatic chemists" from *pneuma*, the Greek word for "air." For example, Joseph Black (1728–1799), working in Scotland in the 1750s, had shown that some substances, those now referred to as "carbonates," contained an air, now known as carbon dioxide, that was heavier than ordinary atmospheric air and did not combust (burn). Soon afterward, the English chemist Henry Cavendish (1731–1810) found that a very light, inflammable air (one that burned easily) was produced when a solution of water and sulfuric acid was poured over iron. Cavendish, who was a firm believer in the phlogiston theory, thought he had isolated pure phlogiston.

Keenly aware of his own ignorance, Lavoisier devoted the whole of 1773 to studying the history of chemistry. He read up on everything that had been written previously about air, or airs, and repeated the experiments of the pneumatic chemists. At first this only succeeded in confusing him. For instance, he came to the conclusion that carbon dioxide (then known as "fixed air") in the atmosphere was responsible for the burning of metals and the increase in their weight.

In 1774, English chemist Joseph Priestley (1733–1804) made an important discovery. Heating oxide of mercury in a closed vessel, he collected a gas ("dephlogisticated air") in which things burned far better than they did in ordinary air. Priestley reported the results of his experiments directly to Lavoisier when he made a visit to Paris that year. As a result of this meeting, Lavoisier carried out a series of experiments of his own. These gradually led him to the realization that this "healthiest and purest part of air," as he called it, was in fact the active agent of burning, the key that unlocked the mystery of combustion.

Experiments with Oxygen

Because the new part of air that Priestley had discovered burned carbon to form the weak acid carbon dioxide, Lavoisier gave it the name "oxygen," which literally means "acid-former" (from the Greek *oxys*, meaning "acid"). He now correctly asserted that combustion occurs when oxygen combines with another substance, releasing (or evolving) heat and light, and causing that substance to increase in weight.

Lavoisier had prepared the ground for a totally new theory of chemistry in which phlogiston played no part. However, it was some years before he spelled out his new theory in full. The chief reason for this was that it remained difficult, without the phlogiston theory, to explain why an inflammable gas was produced when dilute acid was poured on metal. Strangely enough, Lavoisier arrived at the answer to this puzzle through a finding made by Henry Cavendish, the original discoverer of the inflammable gas he believed to be phlogiston.

Repeating an earlier experiment of Joseph Priestley's in 1783–1784, Cavendish found that when a mixture of oxygen and the inflammable gas were exploded by means of an electric spark, moisture covered the sides of the vessel. Cavendish concluded that this was water. To Lavoisier, the experiment was clear evidence that water is made up of parts of oxygen and of Cavendish's inflammable gas. Assisted by Pierre Simon Laplace (1749–1827), Lavoisier demonstrated that when oxygen and the inflammable gas were burned together in a closed vessel, water was formed. Therefore Lavoisier gave this inflammable gas the name "hydrogen," meaning "water-forming." He could now explain why hydrogen was given off when metal was dissolved in dilute acid. It came not from the metal itself (as the phlogistonists claimed) but from the water in the dilute acid as it was broken down into its parts of oxygen and hydrogen.

Revolution in Chemistry

Lavoisier's insight revolutionized chemistry (the science that deals with the composition of substances and the changes they undergo). Since the time of the Greeks, people had believed that all matter was made up of one of four "elements" (earth, air, water, and fire). Lavoisier now rewrote the description of elements, defining them as any substance that cannot be broken down into other substances but out of which all other substances are formed. Hydrogen and oxygen are both elements. They cannot be broken down into simpler substances, nor can they be made by combining other elements. Water, however, is a compound. It is made up of two elements, hydrogen and oxygen, as Lavoisier and Laplace had demonstrated.

By 1785, Lavoisier was confident enough to launch a full attack on the old chemistry. All chemical change could now be explained without resorting to the phlogiston theory. He built up a team of younger assistants around him and held twice-weekly discussions and demonstrations of his latest findings at his home. A new language was needed to describe the processes of chemical change. In 1788,

The solar furnace was designed by Lavoisier in the 1770s. The furnace harnessed the heat of the sun using lenses made from curved sheets of glass that were over 3 feet (1 m) wide.

Lavoisier and his followers founded a journal, *Annals of Chemistry and Physics*, to put across their ideas. The publication still exists today. The following year, in 1789, Lavoisier published *An Elementary Treatise of Chemistry*. Written in clear, logical language, it became the standard textbook on chemistry for many decades.

Arrest and Death

In July 1789, the French Revolution broke out. Anger against the king and the privileged classes had been mounting for years. The government was bankrupt, taxes were higher than ever, and food shortages were widespread, all of which fueled the

Despite his earlier help with the French Revolution, Lavoisier was arrested in 1793. He was sent to the guillotine on May 8, 1794.

fires of rebellion. The overthrow of the old order and the election of a new National Assembly brought about a number of popular reforms.

Lavoisier had supported the early stages of the Revolution, sitting as a political deputy. He wrote a major review of France's finances and agricultural resources, undertook research into the quality of gunpowder, and was part of a committee set up by the Academy of Sciences to create a uniform system of weights and measures. However, the initial unity of the Revolution soon gave way to political division and bitter quarrels. A prime target for hostility were former members of the royal tax-collecting agency, the General Farm. To make matters worse for Lavoisier, only a few years before the Revolution, he was on record for proposing the idea of having a wall around Paris in an effort to curb smuggling.

In November 1793, Lavoisier was arrested, along with other members of the Farm. He might have escaped the death penalty had it not come out at his trial that he had been corresponding with France's political enemies abroad. It was useless to point out that these letters were on scientific matters. He was sentenced to death on May 8, 1794, and was executed that same day. Legend has it that when he asked for a delay in his execution to finish a piece of research, he was told, "The Republic has no need of experts."

In a last letter to his wife, Lavoisier wrote, "I have had a very happy life, and I think I shall be remembered with some regrets and perhaps leave some reputation behind me. What more could I ask?"

The revolutionary leader and failed academician Jean-Paul Marat (above) had put forward accusations against Lavoisier. Marat was assassinated on July 13, 1793, several months before Lavoisier was arrested, but the damage had already been done.

SCIENTIFIC BACKGROUND

Before 1760

Irish physicist and chemist Robert Boyle (1627–1691) and English chemist John Mayow (1640–1679) experiment on air, respiration, and combustion; German chemist Johann Joachim Becher (1635–1682) argues that combustion is due to sulfurous earth

German chemist Georg Stahl (1660–1734) develops phlogiston theory

English chemist Stephen Hales (1677–1761) shows that air is involved in chemical reactions

1760

1763–66 Lavoisier makes a geological tour of France with Jean-Etienne Guettard (1715–1786)

1765

1765 Lavoisier publishes his first scientific paper, on gypsum

1766 English chemist Henry Cavendish (1731–1810) prepares inflammable air (hydrogen)

1768–70 Lavoisier proves that water cannot be changed into earth

1768 Lavoisier is elected to the Academy of Sciences in Paris

1770

1771–72 French chemist Baron Louis Bernard Guyton de Morveau (1737–1816) shows that metals gain weight when burned in air

1771–72 Swedish chemist Carl Wilhelm Scheele (1742–1786) prepares what he calls "fire air," actually oxygen

1772–75 Lavoisier shows that metals burn by absorbing "vital principle" from air

1774 Lavoisier publishes *Opuscles physiques et chimiques*, summarizing his experimentation

1774 English chemist Joseph Priestley (1733–1804) prepares "dephlogisticated air" (oxygen)

1775

1775 Priestley notices that "dew" is formed when hydrogen explodes with oxygen

1776 Lavoisier decides that all acids contain oxygen

1777 Lavoisier develops theory of gaseous state which involves heat as a principle of expansion; identifies "dephlogisticated air" as oxygen

1780

1780 Scheele publishes his book on gases, *Chemical Observations on Air and Fire*

1782 Guyton de Morveau urges a reform of chemical language

1783 Lavoisier shows that water is a compound of hydrogen and oxygen

1784 Lavoisier works with Pierre Simon Laplace (1749–1827) on calorific heat theory and animal heat using guinea pigs

1785

1787 With a group of French chemists, Lavoisier publishes the influential book *Method of Chemical Nomenclature,* which classifies known elements and compounds

1789 Lavoisier publishes his textbook, *Elementary Treatise of Chemistry*

1790

1793 The Academy of Sciences is suppressed as France's Reign of Terror takes hold

1794 Lavoisier is executed on May 8

1794 Priestley emigrates to America after mob attacks his house; he remains a convinced phlogistonist

After 1795

1798 Count Rumford (Benjamin Thompson) (1753–1814) concludes that heat is a kind of motion; he marries Lavoisier's widow in 1804

1802–04 English chemist John Dalton (1766–1844) develops an atomic theory based on Lavoisier's elements

1805 Lavoisier's *Chemical Memoirs* are published posthumously by his widow and collaborator, Marie-Anne Paulze

POLITICAL AND CULTURAL BACKGROUND

1751 The first volume of the *Encyclopedia*, edited by Denis Diderot (1713–1784), is published; it becomes a landmark of the Enlightenment in France

1760 France surrenders Montreal, Canada, to Britain

1762 French philosopher and writer Jean Jacques Rousseau (1712–1778) produces *The Social Contract*; his demand for "Liberty, Equality, and Fraternity" becomes the rallying cry of the French revolutionaries

1768–71 English navigator James Cook (1728–1779) undertakes his first Pacific voyage aboard the *Endeavor*; he is the first European to chart New Zealand and the east coast of Australia

1773 Paul Revere (1735–1818) is among those who take part in the "Boston Tea Party," the destruction of chests of tea at Boston Harbor to protest at the high duties imposed on tea by the British government

1774 Louis XVI, the last prerevolutionary king of France, comes to the throne

1775 Thirteen of Britain's North American colonies rebel against the government of George III, heralding the beginning of the American War of Independence

1778 France intervenes on the side of the colonists against Britain in the American War of Independence

1780 The beginning of the Industrial Revolution in England is marked by the expansion of the cotton industry

1783 The Treaty of Versailles acknowledges the independence of the colonies and the establishment of the United States of America

1784 *Encyclopedia Britannica*, first published 1768–1771, appears in a new 10-volume edition

1789 The French Revolution begins with the storming of the Bastille, the royal prison in Paris which was a hated symbol of royal tyranny. It was found to contain only a handful of prisoners

1793 Louis XVI is tried and executed in Paris, one of more than 2,500 people to be guillotined in Paris during the Reign of Terror

1795, 1807 France captures large parts of Prussia (northern Germany and Poland)

1804 French general Napoleon Bonaparte (1769–1821) crowns himself Emperor of France

Periodic Table of Elements

The periodic table organizes all the chemical elements into a simple chart according to the physical and chemical properties of their atoms. The elements are arranged by atomic number from 1 to 118. The atomic number is based on the number of protons in the nucleus of the atom. The atomic mass is the combined mass of protons and neutrons in the nucleus. Each element has a chemical symbol that is an abbreviation of its name. In some cases, such as potassium, the symbol is an abbreviation of its Latin name ("K" stands for kalium). The name by which the element is commonly known is given in full underneath the symbol. The last item in the box is the atomic mass. This is the average mass of an atom of the element. Scientists have arranged the elements into vertical columns called groups and horizontal rows called periods. Elements in any one group have the same number of electrons in their outer shell and have similar chemical properties. Periods represent the increasing number of electrons it takes to fill the inner and outer shells and become stable. When all the spaces have been filled (Group 18 atoms have all their shells filled), the next period begins.

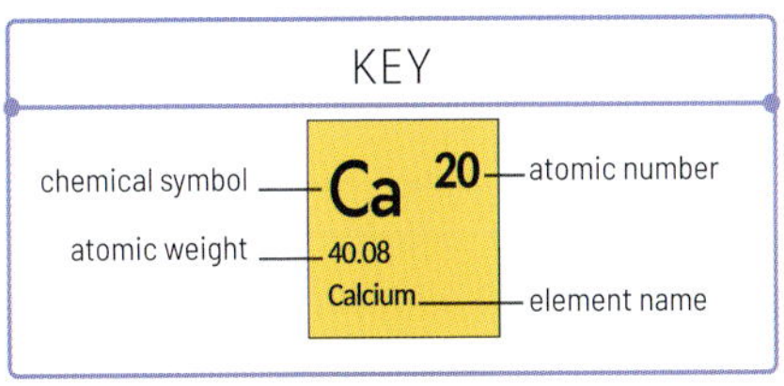

	IIA	IIIB	IVB	VB	VIB	VIIB	VIIIB1	VIIIB2	VIIIB3	IB	IIB	IIIA	IVA	VA	VIA	VIIA	VIIIA
																	He 2 4.003 Helium
	Be 4 9.012 Beryllium											B 5 10.81 Boron	C 6 12.01 Carbon	N 7 14.01 Nitrogen	O 8 16.00 Oxygen	F 9 19.00 Fluorine	Ne 10 20.18 Neon
	Mg 12 24.31 Magnesium											Al 13 26.98 Aluminium	Si 14 28.09 Silicon	P 15 30.97 Phosphorus	S 16 32.06 Sulfur	Cl 17 35.45 Chlorine	Ar 18 39.95 Argon
	Ca 20 40.08 Calcium	Sc 21 44.96 Scandium	Ti 22 47.87 Titanium	V 23 50.94 Vanadium	Cr 24 52 Chromium	Mn 25 54.94 Manganese	Fe 26 55.85 Iron	Co 27 58.93 Cobalt	Ni 28 58.69 Nickel	Cu 29 63.55 Copper	Zn 30 65.38 Zinc	Ga 31 69.72 Gallium	Ge 32 72.63 Germanium	As 33 74.92 Arsenic	Se 34 78.96 Selenium	Br 35 79.90 Bromine	Kr 36 83.80 Krypton
	Sr 38 87.62 Strontium	Y 39 88.91 Yttrium	Zr 40 91.22 Zirconium	Nb 41 92.91 Niobium	Mo 42 95.96 Molybdenum	Tc 43 [98] Technetium	Ru 44 101.1 Ruthenium	Rh 45 102.9 Rhodium	Pd 46 106.4 Palladium	Ag 47 107.9 Silver	Cd 48 112.4 Cadmium	In 49 114.8 Indium	Sn 50 118.71 Tin	Sb 51 121.76 Antimony	Te 52 127.6 Tellurium	I 53 126.9 Iodine	Xe 54 131.3 Xenon
	Ba 56 137.3 Barium	5-71 La-lu Lanthanoids	Hf 72 178.5 Hafnium	Ta 73 180.9 Tantalum	W 74 183.8 Tungsten	Re 75 186.2 Rhenium	Os 76 190.2 Osmium	Ir 77 192.2 Iridium	Pt 78 195.1 Platinum	Au 79 197.0 Gold	Hg 80 200.6 Mercury	Tl 81 204.4 Thallium	Pb 82 207.2 Lead	Bi 83 209 Bismuth	Po 84 [209] Polonium	At 85 [210] Astatine	Rn 86 [222] Radon
	Ra 88 [226] Radium	89-103 Ac-Lr Actinoids	Rf 104 [265] Rutherfordium	Db 105 [268] Dubnium	Sg 106 [266] Seaborgium	Bh 107 [264] Bohrium	Hs 108 [277] Hassium	Mt 109 [276] Meitnerium	Ds 110 [281] Darmstadtium	Rg 111 [280] Roentgenium	Cn 112 [285] Copernicium	Nh 113 [286] Nihonium	Fl 114 [289] Flerovium	Mc 115 [289] Moscovium	Lv 116 [293] Livermorium	Ts 117 [294] Tennessine	Og 118 [294] Oganesson

La 57 138.9 Lanthanum	Ce 58 140.1 Cerium	Pr 59 140.9 Praseodymium	Nd 60 144.2 Neodymium	Pm 61 [145] Promethium	Sm 62 150.4 Samarium	Eu 63 152 Europium	Gd 64 157.3 Gadolinium	Tb 65 158.9 Terbium	Dy 66 162.5 Dysprosium	Ho 67 164.9 Holmium	Er 68 167.3 Erbium	Tm 69 168.9 Thulium	Yb 70 173 Ytterbium	Lu 71 175 Lutetium
Ac 89 [227] Actinium	Th 90 232 Thorium	Pa 91 231 Protactinium	U 92 238 Uranium	Np 93 [237] Neptunium	Pu 94 [244] Plutonium	Am 95 [243] Americium	Cm 96 [247] Curium	Bk 97 [247] Berkelium	Cf 98 [251] Californium	Es 99 [252] Einsteinium	Fm 100 [257] Fermium	Md 101 [258] Mendelevium	No 102 [259] Nobelium	Lr 103 [262] Lawrencium

- Alkali metals
- Alkali earth metals
- Noble gases
- Halogens
- Transition metals
- Lanthanoids
- Actinoids
- Metalloids
- Post transition metals
- Nonmetals

Glossary

acid Substance that dissolves in water to form hydrogen ions (H^+). Acids are neutralized by alkalis and have a pH below 7.

alchemist Person who attempted to change one substance into another using a combination of primitive chemistry and magic.

alkali Substance that dissolves in water to form hydroxide ions (OH^-). Alkalis have a pH greater than 7 and react with acids to form salts.

allotrope A different form of an element in which the atoms are arranged in a different structure.

amorphous Describes something that lacks a definite structure or shape.

atom The smallest independent building block of matter. All substances are made of atoms.

atomic mass The number of protons and neutrons in an atom's nucleus.

atomic number The number of protons in a nucleus.

Avogadro's number The number of atoms, molecules, or ions in one mole of a substance. This number is 602,213,670, 000,000,000,000,000, or 6.0221367×10^{23}.

boiling point The temperature at which a liquid turns into a gas.

bond A chemical connection between atoms.

Boyle's law Gas law which states that the pressure of a gas is inversely proportional to its volume.

Brownian motion Movement of particles suspended in a fluid. The movement is caused by the fluid's molecules colliding with the suspended particles.

capillary action The tendency for liquids to rise up a narrow tube as a result of unequal forces at the water's surface.

Charles's law Gas law which states that the volume of a gas is directly proportional to its temperature.

chemical equation Symbols and numbers that show how reactants change into products during a chemical reaction.

chemical formula The letters and numbers that represent a chemical compound, such as "H_2O" for water.

chemical reaction The reaction of two or more chemicals (the reactants) to form new chemicals (the products).

chemical symbol The letters that represent a chemical, such as "Cl" for chlorine or "Na" for sodium.

compound Substance made from more than one element that has undergone a chemical reaction.

compress To reduce in size or volume by squeezing or exerting pressure.

concentration The quantity of solute in a given amount of solvent.

condensation The change of state from a gas to a liquid.

conductor A substance that carries electricity and heat.

covalent bond Bond in which atoms share one or more electrons.

critical point The temperature and pressure at which a substance can exist in all three phases—solid, liquid, and gas.

crystal A solid made of regular repeating patterns of atoms.

crystal lattice The arrangement of atoms in a crystalline solid.

density The mass of substance in a unit of volume.

dipole attraction The attractive force between the electrically charged ends of molecules.

dissolve To form a solution.

elastic collision Collision during which no energy is lost.

electricity A stream of electrons or other charged particles moving through a substance.

electrolyte Liquid containing ions that carries a current between electrodes.

electron A tiny negatively charged particle that moves around the nucleus of an atom.

element A material that cannot be broken up into simpler ingredients via a chemical reaction. Elements contain only one type of atom.

energy level Electrons are arranged in shells around an atom's nucleus. These shells represent different energy levels. Those closest to the nucleus have the lowest energy.

evaporation The change of state from a liquid to a gas when the liquid is at a temperature below its boiling point.

fission Process by which a large atom breaks up into two or more smaller fragments.

fusion When small atoms fuse to make a single larger atom.

gas State in which particles are not joined and are free to move in any direction.

heat The transfer of energy between atoms. Adding heat makes atoms move more quickly.

heat capacity The amount of heat required to change the temperature of an object by 1 degree Celsius (1.8°F).

heat of fusion The amount of energy needed to turn a solid into a liquid.

heat of vaporization The amount of energy needed to turn a liquid into a gas.

heterogeneous mixture A mixture in which different substances are spread unevenly throughout.

homogeneous mixture A mixture in which one substance has dissolved or been completely mixed into another.

hydrogen bond A weak dipole attraction that always involves a hydrogen atom.

hydrolysis The process by which a molecule splits after reacting with a molecule of water.

hydrophilic Describes a thing that has an attraction to water.

hydrophobic Describes a thing that is repelled by water.

immiscibility When two or more liquids do not mix but form separate layers.

insoluble When a substance cannot dissolve in a solvent.

intermolecular bonds The forces that attract molecules to one another. These bonds are weaker than those between atoms in a molecule.

intramolecular bond Strong bond between atoms in a molecule.

ion An atom that has lost or gained one or more electrons.

ionic bond The attraction between positive and negative ions in an ionic compound.

ionization The formation of ions by adding or removing electrons from atoms.

isotope Atoms of a given element have the same number of protons but can have different numbers of neutrons. These different versions of the same element are called isotopes.

kinetic energy The energy of movement.

kinetic theory The study of heat flow and other processes in terms of the motion of the atoms and molecules involved.

liquid Substance in which particles are loosely bonded and are able to move freely around each other.

malleable Describes a material that can be hammered into different shapes without breaking. Metals are malleable.

matter Anything that can be weighed.

melting point The temperature at which a solid changes into a liquid. When a liquid changes into a solid, this same temperature is also called the freezing point.

metal An element that is solid, shiny, malleable, ductile, and conductive.

metallic bond Bond in which outer electrons are free to move in the spaces between the atoms.

metalloid Elements that have properties of both metals and nonmetals.

mixture Matter made from different types of substances that are not physically or chemically bonded together.

molality The number of moles of solute dissolved in one kilogram of solvent.

molarity The number of moles of solute dissolved in one liter of solvent.

mole The amount of any substance that contains the same number of atoms as in 12 grams of carbon-12 atoms. This number is 6.022×10^{23}.

molecule Two or more bonded atoms that form a substance with specific properties.

mole fraction The ratio of the number of moles of one substance to the total moles of all the substances present.

neutron One of the particles that make up the nucleus of an atom. Neutrons do not have any electric charge.

nucleus The central part of an atom. The nucleus contains protons and neutrons. The exception is hydrogen, which contains only one proton.

phase change A change from one state to another.

photon A particle that carries a quantity of energy, such as in the form of light.

plasma Fourth state of matter in which atoms have lost some or all of their electrons.

precipitate An insoluble solid formed by a double displacement reaction between two dissolved compounds.

pressure The force produced by pressing on something.

product The new substance or substances created by a chemical reaction.

proton A positively charged particle in an atom's nucleus.

reactants The ingredients necessary for a chemical reaction.

relative atomic mass A measure of the mass of an atom compared with the mass of another atom. The values used are the same as those for atomic mass.

relative molecular mass The sum of all the atomic masses of the atoms in a molecule.

salt A compound made from positive and negative ions that forms when an alkali reacts with an acid.

shell The orbit of an electron. Each shell can contain a specific number of electrons and no more.

solid State of matter in which particles are held in a rigid arrangement.

solute A substance that dissolves in a solvent.

solution A mixture of two or more elements or compounds in a single phase (solid, liquid, or gas).

solvent A liquid that dissolves a solute.

specific heat capacity The amount of heat required to change the temperature of a specified amount of a substance by 1°C (1.8°F).

standard conditions Normal room temperature and pressure.

state The form that matter takes—either a solid, a liquid, or a gas.

subatomic particles Particles that are smaller than an atom.

supercooled liquid A liquid that has been cooled below its freezing point but has not changed into a solid.

temperature A measure of how fast molecules are moving.

valence electrons The electrons in the outer shell of an atom.

van der Waals forces Short-lived forces between atoms and molecules.

viscous Describes a liquid that is not very runny and flows slowly.

volatile Describes a liquid that evaporates easily.

volume The space that a solid, liquid, or gas occupies.

Further Information

American Association for the Advancement of Science
1200 New York Avenue NW
Washington, DC 20005
(202) 326-6400
Website: www.aaas.org
This international nonprofit organization is dedicated to advancing science around the world by serving as an educator, leader, spokesperson, and professional association.

American Museum of Natural History
200 Central Park West
New York, NY 10024-5102
(212) 769-5100
Website: www.amnh.org
The museum showcases hundreds of animal species and fossils from the history of life on Earth.

L.R. Ingersoll Physics Museum
1150 University Avenue
Madison, WI 53706-1390
(608) 262-1137
Website: www.physics.wisc.edu/ingersollmuseum/
This museum offers a hands-on experience in physics.

New York Hall of Science
47-01 111th Street
Corona, NY 11368
(718) 699-0005
Website: www.nysci.org
This innovative science museum allows visitors to play and interact with science.

The Science Museum
Exhibition Road
South Kensington
SW7 2DD
London, England
033-0058-0058
Website: www.sciencemuseum.org.uk
The Science Museum is renowned for its collections, galleries, and exhibitions dedicated to science.

Society of Physics Students
American Institute of Physics
1 Physics Ellipse
College Park, MD 20740
(301) 209-3007
Website: www.spsnational.org
This society unites physics students across the United States, encouraging communication and education in the field of physics.

Books

Biskup, Agnieszka. *The Solid Truth about States of Matter with Max Axiom, Super Scientist*. Mankato, MN: Capstone Publishing 2019.

Braun, Eric. *Curious Pearl Explains States of Matter*. Mankato, MN: Capstone Publishing, 2018.

Congdon, Lisa. *The Illustrated Encyclopedia of the Elements: The Powers, Uses and Histories of Every Atom in the Universe.* San Francisco, CA: Chronicle Books, 2021.

Demtröder, Wolfgang. *Atoms, Molecules and Photons: An Introduction to Atomic, Molecular, and Quantum Physics.* Switzerland: Springer Nature, 2019.

Dorling Kindersley. *The Chemistry Book.* London, UK. Dorling Kindersley, 2022.

Fleisher, Paul. *Liquids and Gases: Principles of Fluid Mechanics*. London, UK: Living Book Press, 2019.

Gray, Theodore and Mann, Nick. *Molecules: The Elements and the Architecture of Everything*. New York, NY: Black Dog and Leventhal, 2018.

Linde, Barbara Martina. *Atoms: It Matters*. New York, NY: Rosen Publishing 2020.

Lowe, Derek B. *The Chemistry Book: From Gunpowder to Graphene, 250 Milestones in the History of Chemistry.* New York, NY: Union Square and Co, 2022.

Moore, John T. *Chemistry Essentials for Dummies*. London, UK: For Dummies, 2019.

Morris Parker, Bertha. *Matter, Molecules and Atoms*. New York, NY: Yesterday's Classics, 2018.

NEDU. *Chemistry Made Easy: An Illustrated Study Guide for Students To Easily Learn Chemistry*. Cheyenne, WY: NEDU LLC, 2021.

Nguyen-Kim, Mai Thi and Lenkova, Claire. *Chemistry for Breakfast*. Vancouver, Canada: Greystone Books, 2022.

Post, Richard et al. *Chemistry: Concepts and Problems, A Self Teaching Guide.* Hoboken, NJ: John Wiley, 2020.

Scientific American. *Ask the Experts: Chemistry*. New York, NY: Rosen Publishing 2018.

Sezer, Ali O. Chemistry: *An Illustrated Guide for All Ages*. New York, NY: Barron's, 2021.

Shores, Lorie. *How to Make a Liquid Rainbow*. Mankato, MN: Capstone Publishing, 2018.

Smithsonian. *The Elements Book: A Visual Encyclopedia of the Periodic Table.* New York, NY: Dorling Kindersley, 2017.

Sterling Education. *High School Chemistry: Comprehensive Content for High-School Chemistry*. New York, NY: Sterling Education, 2022.

Index

G

H

I

K

L

M

Photo Credits

Front Cover: Shutterstock: Putan Cornel.

DeAgostini Picture Library: G. Dagli Orti 80; **Getty Images:** BSIP/UIG 71, Hulton Archive/Apic 22, Hulton Archive/Imagno 74, Photo Researchers/Charles D Winters 31l; **iStock:** marccophoto 58; **Mary Evans Picture Library:** Imageworks 79; **Science Source:** Andrew Lambert Photography 41, Photo Researchers 72, SPL 78; **Shutterstock:** Africa Studio 3, 36, aslysun 57, baranq 42, BlueBarronPhoto 46, Javier Crespo 66, dinadesign 65b, J.A Dunbar 45, Randa Firoica 48, Zelinska Gamma 28, B. Godart 15, Alexander Hadji 27, hedgehog94 29, Igor Hotinsky 19, Imagentle 23, Jforensic 39, Albert Karimov 51, KPixMining 62, Mike Ledray 60, likingthings 6, megaflopp 12, mineral-vision 7, Luciano Mortula 54, mountainpix 53, New Africa 34, 37, Don Pablo 26, Alessander Proshkin 52, Zelijko Radojko 55, Alexander Raths 9, Piotr Snigorski 47, Kuttelvaserova Stuchelova 50, Surked 69, Kan Taengnuanjan 13, Vixit 24, voan 31r, Wavebreak Media 40, Jack White 32, M.G. White 65t, Dima Zel 14; **Thinkstock:** Goodshoot 63.

All other photography and artwork Brown Bear Books.

Brown Bear Books has made every attempt to contact the copyright holder. Please email licensing@brownbearbooks.co.uk with any information about omissions.